JUDSON PRESS
PUBLISHERS SINCE 1824

Missional
PREACHING
Engage ∎ Embrace ∎ Transform

AL TIZON

Foreword by Christine Aroney-Sine
Afterword by Wallace Charles Smith

JUDSON PRESS
PUBLISHERS SINCE 1824
VALLEY FORGE, PA

Missional Preaching: Engage • Embrace • Transform
© 2012 by Judson Press, Valley Forge, PA 19482-0851
All rights reserved.

Unless otherwise noted, Bible quotations in this volume are from the New Revised Standard Version of the Bible, copyright © 1989 by the Division of Christian Education of the National Council of the Churches of Christ in the United States of America. Used by permission. All rights reserved.

Other Scriptures are quoted from:
HOLY BIBLE: *New International Version*, copyright © 1973, 1978, 1984. Used by permission of Zondervan Bible Publishers. (NIV)
The Holy Bible, King James Version. (KJV)
The New King James Version. Copyright © 1972, 1984 by Thomas Nelson Inc. (NKJV)
The *Holy Bible,* New Living Translation, copyright © 1996, 2004. Used by permission of Tyndale House Publishers, Inc., Wheaton, IL 60189. All rights reserved. (NLT)

Interior design by Beth Oberholtzer.
Cover design by Hampton Design Group.

Library of Congress Cataloging-in-Publication data

Tizon, Al.
　　Missional preaching : engage, embrace, transform / Al Tizon ; foreword by Christine Aroney-Sine ; afterword by Wallace Charles Smith. — 1st ed.
　　　　p.　cm.
　　ISBN 978-0-8170-1704-0 (pbk. : alk. paper) 1. Preaching. 2. Mission of the church. I. Title.
　　BV4221.T59 2012
　　251—dc23

2011044880

Printed in the U.S.A.
First Edition, 2012.

CONTENTS

FOREWORD

How do we preach and teach missionally? Many of us grapple with this question as we seek to share the Word of God and mobilize God's people to be world changers. God's Word is meant to transform not just us but also the world in which we live. Could it be that one reason many churches in the West seem to be dying is because they are not hearing God's transforming, missional word?

In this book Al Tizon contends that our problem is not right doctrine or even right practice but rather the integration of the two. We have not allowed the *missio Dei* (mission of God) to permeate our beings. We have not read the whole of the Bible from Genesis to Revelation with missional eyes. We have not taken the mission of God seriously for all of life, so we have not worked very hard to incorporate mission into the regular experience of our churches.

I believe a church that does not practice what it preaches will soon die. I often tell people that I learned my theology in the refugee camps on the Thai–Cambodian border, because it was there that what I'd heard preached over the years moved from my head to my heart. My experiences working with the displaced and marginalized moved me from a passive pew-sitter to a radical activist.

Al, too, is both a theologian and a practitioner, and his passion— for a church that is fully missional, not just in word but also in deed— is obvious throughout the pages of this book. His desire is to help followers of Jesus integrate what they hear on Sunday with the way they live during the rest of the week. In this book he has drawn not only from his own experience and theological knowledge but also from a rich and diverse group of other preachers and practitioners.

We are all called to be God's people, to join together in transforming a world that is sorely in need of the love of God, yet so many in our congregation have virtually no engagement with the world outside the church doors. The most dynamic movements within the Western church today are those that encourage the integration of preaching and mission. Missional churches that are transforming their neighborhoods; missional communities that live with the poor and work from the inside to rejuvenate their communities; multicultural churches that model something of the transnational nature of the kingdom of God— all these are exciting examples of what God is doing.

When our preaching and teaching flow out of the convictions of a transformed heart, it is amazing to see what can happen. Churches come to life as they recognize the need for this type of integration and begin to look beyond the church building to the needy world outside. Preaching is not just about words but also about action. When we learn to preach in ways that help galvanize congregations into action, we will once again have a body of Christ that brings transformation to our world.

Christine Aroney-Sine
Executive Director of Mustard Seed Associates
Seattle, WA

PREFACE

The most horrifying thought in writing a book on preaching is that I might come across as saying, "I know how to preach; let me show you how." The fact is, my own preaching experience over the years has included its share of fumbling, stuttering, fighting off butterflies, saying the wrong things, overconfidence, underconfidence, lack of preparedness, doubt, insecurity, and other homiletical pitfalls. So I am probably not qualified to write a how-to manual on preaching, even if I'd wanted to.

The idea for this book emerged several years ago when I searched in vain for a basic text to help me frame a seminary course on missional preaching. I found many books on preaching, and a growing number of books on the missional church, but my search did not uncover a single volume that satisfactorily combined the two. Some of the missional church books had sections that dealt specifically with church leadership (and, therefore, preaching), and there were books on preaching that touched on missional themes. But, I thought to myself, the integral relationship between mission and biblical preaching warrants a more in-depth treatment than a sentence or two here and a paragraph there.

I love the church—despite its blemishes, imperfections, and short-comings. I credit the various communities of faith with which I have been involved throughout my Christian life for nurturing, growing, challenging, and equipping me to be all that God has called me to be. Much of the credit for this goes to the pastor-teachers of these churches who faithfully studied the Scriptures and fed the sheep with stimulating, life-changing, church-shaping, community-transforming—in a word, biblical—truth. For me, there is nothing like the Word preached excellently by which God has regularly rocked my world.

Like most of you I have sat through plenty of bad sermons. But on those occasions when the Word of God has gotten through, I've been forever changed. Over time, I have discovered that my own spiritual gift set includes preaching and teaching. This has led to a life of serving various churches in the United States and the Philippines over the past twenty years, in a variety of roles including guest preacher, interim pastor, associate pastor, small group leader, senior pastor, seminar and workshop leader, and now seminary professor.

As God's Word has shaped me (as both listener and proclaimer), I have developed another love—a love for the world that God has made and so loves. It is this Spirit-breathed love for the world that has catapulted me into a life of mission, engaging in community development in the Philippines for nine years, first in the slums of Manila and then in a rural province north of Manila that was devastated by the infamous 1991 eruption of Mt. Pinatubo.[1] Today, I participate in God's mission in the United States as director of Word & Deed Network (WDN), a ministry of Evangelicals for Social Action that seeks to help local churches engage their communities in holistic ministries. The desire to bear witness to the gospel by both word and deed and to point the way for all to experience the bounty of the kingdom of God has defined my reason for being, even as I myself am broken and in daily need of God's grace.

So these two loves reside in my person: (1) love for the church with a special heartthrob for the holistic proclamation of the Word, and (2) love for the world, which God longs to redeem. It is primarily these two loves, and not just because I needed a textbook for a course on missional preaching, that have ultimately inspired me to write this book.

Undertaking this project has helped me know a little more about myself; for in retrospect, I see that most if not all of my preaching and teaching has had the pervasive influence of mission in it. By that I don't mean *all* my sermons have been about mission, but rather that every topic I have tackled—be it stewardship, love, discipleship, prayer, or whatever—seems to have had mission integrally intertwined throughout. I recently found a short homily I gave at a wedding in which I encouraged the couple to understand their marriage as a window through which people can see the love of God for all. The audacity, some might say, of preaching mission at a wedding! I hope that I appropriately maintained the celebratory nature of marital love; but I did encourage a type of marital love that looked beyond itself to a greater love, God's love for all. I am open to the charge of tunnel vision, but something tells me that God's mission can and should determine our Christian worship in some fundamental way, whether at a Sunday service, a wedding, a baptism, or a funeral.

What would happen if God's mission began to permeate every fiber of the church's being? What kind of preaching would serve such a process? What might something called "missional preaching" sound like? As this book addresses such questions, I trust that those of us who preach and teach will gain a better grasp of our crucial role in shaping the church into the image of God and God's mission.

NOTE

1. For a short account of one of the most destructive volcanic eruptions of the twentieth century, go to "The Cataclysmic 1991 Eruptions of Mt. Pinatubo, Philippines." http://pubs.usgs.gov/fs/1997/fs113-97/ (accessed August 10, 2011).

* * *

Dear Lord, you have sent me into this world to preach your word. So often the problems of the world seem so complex and intricate that your word strikes me as embarrassingly simple. . . . Do not allow evil powers to seduce me with the complexities of the world's problems, but give me the strength to think clearly, speak freely, and act boldly in your service. Give me the courage to show the dove in a world so full of serpents. Amen.[1]

NOTE

1. Excerpted from Henri J. M. Nouwen, "A Preacher's Prayer," in *Seeds of Hope: A Henri Nouwen Reader,* ed. Robert Durback (New York City: Image Books, 1997), 112.

ACKNOWLEDGMENTS

Books are almost never solo projects. I feel compelled to begin my list of thanks by acknowledging the pastors in my life through whom I've received nourishment for my journey these past three-plus decades. I am eternally grateful to each of you—you know who you are—for literally speaking into my life. Three professors also stick out in my mind—Murray Dempster, Byron Klaus, and Doug Petersen, all at Vanguard University of Southern California in my formative years. They taught me how to preach by example. They were not my homiletics professors, but each time I heard them speak—whether it be in chapel, or in a church service, or sometimes they would break out in class—they hypnotized me with Spirit-filled, passionate preaching. "If I could just be half that compelling . . . ," I would say to myself.

Fast forwarding to the here-and-now, I wish to thank the students of my missional preaching course, which I regularly teach here at Palmer Theological Seminary. Their questions, insights, and experiences have made for lively, relevant discussions that, in retrospect, have provided the on-the-ground substance for this book. One former student in particular, the Reverend Tracy Saletta, deserves special thanks for providing helpful feedback on the manuscript. Thank you, Tracy! Special thanks also go to Palmer MDiv students Marcos Ortega and David Michaux, who provided much-needed nuts-and-bolts, behind-the-scenes detail work to make this book happen. Thanks also to Steve Munz, associate pastor of City Line Church in Philadelphia at the time, who helped tremendously by doing some preliminary research in the early stages of this project.

A few years ago, it was my honor to deliver the Westerdahl Lectures at North Park Theological Seminary in Chicago, where I went public for the first time with this material. The positive feedback and

stimulating questions from both faculty and students not only inspired me to develop the material into book form but also helped
shape the content in significant ways. Thank you to then-President
and Dean Jay Phelan, Professor Soong-Chan Rah, and the rest of the
NPTS faculty who all made me feel at home. Many thanks as well to
Guylla Brown, administrator extraordinaire, who took good care of
me by attending to all of the behind-the-scenes details.

My colleagues at Evangelicals for Social Action and Palmer Seminary have encouraged me more than they know to be "my holistic
self." This encouragement to be all I can be enables me to take on a
book such as this with confidence. In my mind, without such a community from which to launch, a book like this cannot happen.

Many played direct roles in the making of this book. Early on I
asked a team of friends to give their feedback on chapters; heaven
forbid if I try to present anything unfiltered by the wisdom of these
friends. Also a huge "Thank You" must go to each preacher friend
who contributed a sermon to this project. Like I told each of you personally, your sermons have upped the quality of this book by leaps
and bounds. Rebecca Irwin-Diehl and the other good folks at Judson
Press gave me much encouragement and confidence by taking on this
project with me. Thanks for taking a chance, Judson.

Immeasurable thanks go to my wife, Janice, and to our four children. This is not just an obligatory way to end the Acknowledgments
section; on the contrary, they have been my best preaching critics
through the years. They were (and continue to be) my real homeliti-
cal teachers, as I take very seriously their honest criticisms, as well
as their affirmation and praise. Their feedback—ranging from "You
didn't explain that very well" to "You were anointed this morning"
to "Stop rocking on your toes so much" to "You're easy to listen
to"—has encouraged and corrected me like no other. More importantly, they help me to practice what I preach like no other. Thanks,
family, for keeping me honest!

Al Tizon
Palmer Theological Seminary of Eastern University
Wynnewood, PA

INTRODUCTION

Important. Substantive. Inspiring. Relevant. As preachers and teach-ers, we desire to be all these things. We work hard at it. And yet, let's face it: We are too often like Father McKenzie, "writing the words of a sermon that no one will hear; no one comes near . . ."[1]

Ministers deal with the problem of irrelevance in different ways. Some ignore it and hope—naïvely, desperately—that the Word-of-God-will-not-return-void cliché is true: "God's Word will get through in spite of us." Some go seminar-hopping in search of fresh new approaches to the ancient art. Still others choose to abandon the practice of preaching altogether—at least, as it has been done traditionally—in favor of sharing, dialoging, asking, and facilitating (more on this shortly).

Such efforts point to the sincere attempt to keep the gospel relevant and alive for God's people. After all, for those whose task is to educate, inspire, and equip God's people by "the greatest story ever told," it borders on sin to bore people with the gospel! If this is even slightly true, then preachers across the land, including myself, undoubtedly transgress on a regular basis.

Equating sermonic boredom with sin obviously exaggerates the point, especially in light of the burden placed upon pastors to offer sermons that are at once witty, creative, practical, exegetically accurate, socially relevant, and intellectually stimulating—Sunday in and Sunday out. To do so amid the weekly demands of congregational care, committee meetings, conflict management, and administrative duties deserves not criticism and scorn, but a plate of fresh-baked cookies, a spa or restaurant certificate, and other gifts of grace and encouragement. But few would disagree that something has gone terribly wrong if the feast of the gospel results in spiritual malnourishment and dehydration. Notorious culprits of such preaching famines include ill-preparation, uninspired delivery, marathon speaking, highfalutin theologizing, and contextual ignorance.

The Problem: Content, Not Method

These and other related culprits, however, belong primarily to the category of method, which I believe fails to address the root of the crisis. I argue in this book that the root cause of lifeless sermons—which ultimately produce lifeless churches—is the lack of missional substance. By "substance" I do not mean that these sermons lack right doctrine; they may or may not. I mean that they lack awareness of the very reality that gives ultimate meaning to the church—namely, the *missio Dei*, the mission of God. The homiletical crisis in our churches is not ultimately a method problem but a content problem. If scholars such as Lesslie Newbigin, David Bosch, Arthur Glasser, and Christopher Wright are correct when they say that the whole Bible—and not just selected passages—is a missionary book, then to preach from the Bible without any reference to mission surely misses the mark.[2]

Darrell Guder and his colleagues at the Gospel in Our Culture Network (GOCN) have played a large role in catalyzing the missional church movement in North America. In their 1998 book, *The Missional Church,* Guder and his coauthors claim that "the crisis of the . . . church will not be found at the level of method and problem solving. . . . The real issues are spiritual and theological."[3] Their call to be missional, therefore, was and is not so much a call to change the way we do things (although we probably *do* need to change the way we do things!), but rather a call to understand anew what it means to be the church of Jesus Christ. "It has to do with who we are," Guder and his colleagues continue, "and what we are for."[4]

Just as the question of the crisis in the church as a whole is not *how,* but *who* and *why,* so it is for preaching in particular. To be sure, there is always room for improvement with regard to delivery, and this book does not completely skirt the methodological question (see Appendix, "Is It Missional—A Sermon Evaluation Form"). But questions of method will not get at the crux of the homiletical crisis, especially for this postmodern generation that seeks authenticity more demandingly than previous generations. The question is not primarily, "How should we preach?" but rather, "Why and to whom do we preach?"

God's Mission to God's People

We proclaim to a people redeemed by a missional God. As those called to preach and teach, we have been given the task, among many others, of shaping the redeemed community by the Word to conform to the image of this God. Central to this task is the understanding of mission as part of God's very nature and therefore a part of the church's very nature. "In proposing a new theological perspective on mission," writes homiletics professor Eunjoo Mary Kim, "I remember that the mission of the church is grounded in the nature and missionary activity of the triune God."[5] God's nature as Trinity—as harmonious community and self-giving love—has a built-in invitation to creation and all its inhabitants to experience *shalom*—the all-encompassing reality of peace, unity, love, and glory, all of which are inherent within the trinitarian Godhead. "As God is the missionary God," Kim continues, "the church is a missionary community," inviting all to experience life in the kingdom of God.[6] We will discuss the *missio Dei* in more detail in chapter 1. For now, suffice it to say that God's people desperately need to reclaim their missional identity, and I contend that much of the responsibility to secure this identity lies on those who "rightly divide the word of truth," that is, those who preach and teach in and for the church.

When we don't preach missionally—that is, when the sense of God's mission does not drive our proclamation—then the purpose of sermonizing becomes primarily to build up the fellowship of believers. This is not so much wrong as it is woefully incomplete. At best, preaching solely to and for the body creates "the family church," in which people genuinely care for one another, but also in which that care extends only to those who belong to the inner circle. At worst, "building up the fellowship of believers" serves as a euphemism for making parishioners feel secure and comfortable in this life, as if security and comfort were the ultimate goals of Christian discipleship. But God, whose very triune being defines community and love, created us in a way that we can be fulfilled only insofar as we look beyond ourselves. Leo Tolstoy wrote toward the end of his life, "I know now that people only *seem* to live when they care only for themselves, and that it is by love for others that they truly live."[7] Jesus said it more succinctly: "Those who lose their life for my sake, and for the sake of the gospel, will save it" (Mark 8:35).

Furthermore, missional preaching cannot be relegated to specially designated Missions Sundays and holidays; mission must be the energy that motivates *every* Sunday. Otherwise we send a subliminal message that "normal" Sundays are primarily for the internal concerns of the household of faith. To be missional calls for a reversal of priorities: Instead of one or two annual Missions Sundays, we should have one or two "Church Sundays" each year where the service intentionally focuses inward! As for "normal Sundays" throughout the year, we preach mission in order to guide, inspire, equip, and challenge God's people to live their lives worthy of the call to transform the world.

Insofar as pastors cater to an insular model of church through their preaching, they will find their own creative tanks empty and eventually will preach out of their perceived obligation to coddle their parishioners. Sermons devoid of mission make for church members devoid of vitality, energy, and sense of purpose. By way of contrast, year-round sermons saturated in the richness of God's mission make for church members—no, *disciples*—who pulsate with life, energy, and commitment to the higher purposes of God. This book seeks to deepen and enliven the church's preaching, not necessarily by offering a new homiletic, but by renewing our understanding of biblical mission.

Missional Preaching: Basic Assumptions

Missional preaching is built upon two basic assumptions. First, *mission is integral to what it means to be the church*. To invoke Emil Brunner's famous metaphor, "The church exists by mission just as fire exists by burning. Where there is no mission, there is no church."[8] This does not mean there is nothing if there is no mission; it just means that whatever exists in our congregations is not the church. It might be a social club, a religio-civic institution, or even a large extended family of loving people. But without that outward looking gaze, without that larger, beyond-itself purpose, without that Christ-centered, Spirit-inspired vision for global transformation—in a word, without *mission*—we fall short of biblical *ekklesia*, a community of Christ's disciples.

A second assumption is that *biblical preaching remains one of the primary ways in which leaders influence God's people and shape the church*. Guder and colleagues are right to point out that the common use of the term *preaching* nowadays "has . . . come to mean something quite different from the New Testament definition of the word."[9] Whereas the preaching of the apostles occurred as a public announcement of the good news for all to hear—from the lowly in society to those in high office and everyone in between—preaching today "bears more resemblance to the New Testament concept of teaching" in that it is "practiced only within the church, to the faithful, on Sunday morning."[10] To attempt to recover the original New Testament use of *keryssein* (preach), however, would detract from the goal of this book. For our purposes, preaching and teaching are close enough in practical meaning that I use them here interchangeably. Missional preaching, therefore, is not directed toward the world-at-large; it is for the people of God in the context of the world-at-large. Like the Sermon on the Mount, where Jesus spoke directly to the Twelve but within earshot of everyone else present (Matt. 5:1-2), missional preaching addresses God's people while never losing sight of the world surrounding them. Missional preaching is teaching as if the world matters.

Despite the postmodern suspicion surrounding symbols of authority (such as the pulpit and preacher), the proclaimed word of God—the *kerygma*—still guides, shapes, corrects, and transforms. Even those who have denounced traditional preaching—I think particularly of some within the emerging/emergent church movement— must concede that words still matter. The gospel, after all, is good *news,* and as church leaders, to articulate the good news is an integral part of our vocation. True, the Word must be lived and activated and seen in the lives of those who proclaim it. True, the onus is on church leaders to find new ways to speak it effectively. And true, a community of authentic relationships provides the proper context for interpretation. If postmodern times, for example, necessitate a more nuanced delivery in the form of questioning, self-discovery, facilitation, or what emergent pastor Doug Pagitt calls "progressional dialogue,"[11] then more power to the emerging experimenters of the Word.

But these approaches to addressing the crisis in the church's preaching are primarily methodological. And, as I have already asserted, method is not the root problem. A new, more inclusive, dialogical, religiously correct way to communicate the gospel is not what I mean by missional preaching. *Missional* describes a people who have been so gripped by the biblical vision of God's *shalom* for the world that it permeates all that they do, say, and think. Preaching—however way we choose to do it—is indispensable in disciple-making—that is, in shaping God's people to conform to the image of their missional God.

These two basic assumptions—(1) *mission is integral to the church's identity,* and (2) *preaching plays a central role in shaping that identity*—warrant the need to understand something called missional preaching.

Making Sense of the Missional Morass

Prior to the publication of Guder's *Missional Church* in 1998, terms such as *mission, missions, missionary,* and even *missiological* all had secure places in the church lexicon. But *missional*—is that even a word? Like many others, I have had to add the term to my computer's spell-checker so the annoying red squiggly line that indicates a spelling error won't show up every time I type it. But despite not quite being a "real" word, *missional* has been used (and perhaps even overused) for the last decade or so. As homiletics professor John Dally notes, "Although [it] has not yet made the big-time dictionaries, a Web search for 'missional' yields 864,000 hits . . . . About 800,000 of those entries seem to be defending the word's existence."[12] Official or not then, *missional* has caught on and is being utilized extensively. How it has become an indelible part of church-speak in a matter of a little more than a decade attests to just how unknowingly deprived God's people have been for a fresh, genuine sense of mission.

However, the popularity of *missional* does not mean that those utilizing the term do so in the same way. In fact, I suspect many groups employing the word are not even aware of GOCN's twelve original indicators of a missional church.[13] Rather than GOCN's understanding of the term serving as a kind of regulating gateway, the word *missional* seems to have irreversibly broken the dam, as churches and organizations across the land claim the term to describe their own versions of renewed commitment to outreach. Guder himself notes, "The word has taken on a life of its own."[14]

This development could indicate the wonderfully unpredictable movements of the Spirit. But it could also point to the lamentable loss of theological depth that the original GOCN leaders warned against. I suspect they would cry foul if *missional* were to devolve into a mere synonym for *strategic* or *practical.* Reducing it to the pragmatic level would not only violate the term; it would do an injustice to the movement. Referring to one of the seminal books authored by the GOCN leaders, Lois Barrett quips, "It is not a 'how-to-become-a-successful-church' book, with an easy three-step process for becoming missional."[15] Barrett's words should serve as a general warning to any church or group that is tempted to strip the term *missional* of its theological substance.

Amid the morass of the many denominations, churches, and organizations that use the term, how can we make cohesive sense of the missional movement? Intentional or not, respected cultural interpreter Tom Sine has provided a concise overview of the missional movement in his book *The New Conspirators,* by identifying four streams of contemporary expressions of church mission.[16]

These four streams—emerging, missional, mosaic, and monastic—flow separately enough to distinguish them from one another; yet they also cross at certain junctures and converge to constitute the missional movement as a whole—this, despite one of them specifically donning the "missional" label. While the specific missional stream refers primarily to church renewal efforts occurring within traditional mainline churches, the four streams together create the larger missional movement. All four streams are undeniably missional, and representatives of each would describe themselves as such.

The common denominator in the four streams is the life-giving water of the kingdom of God that flows through them, a flow that moves outward in order to bring healing, wholeness, and sustenance to creation and all of its inhabitants. Space will not allow me to discuss here the multitudinous lists of characteristics, marks, elements, indicators, patterns, and so on that have been offered to define the missional church. Suffice it to say, at the risk of oversimplification, that to be missional ultimately means to exist in order to bring life— the life only God in Christ can give—to others. (I will offer a more detailed definition after looking more carefully at the four streams.)

Each of these four streams—emerging, missional, mosaic, and monastic—brings particular strengths to what it means to be missional. The emerging stream, with its emphasis on innovative ways to relate to God, one another (as the people of God), and the community at large, stresses the importance of relational authenticity in mission. Those who swim in this stream—primarily a younger generation of white (and, increasingly, Asian American) evangelicals in the United Kingdom and the United States—take postmodern culture seriously.

As such, emergent Christians are driven at once by a holy discontent with traditional forms of church and a renewed desire to bear witness to Jesus incarnationally—that is, in genuine relationships with those generally unwelcomed by conventional church: the sinner, the worldly, the atheist, the person of another faith, the poor.

The (specific) missional stream, with its emphasis upon the theological inseparability of God, church, and mission, stresses the importance of the church's self-understanding—its very identity—as rooted in Christ and Christ's purposes. As such, the church exists as both the fruit and extension of God's mission. The church does not just send out missionaries to faraway lands; the church, as it is situated in a specific context, is sent by God to *be* good news in its surroundings. Those who swim here—mostly an older, educated generation of Protestant mainliners who are committed to renewal—"challenge primarily traditional churches to focus more outwardly in mission and to rediscover their calling as 'God's sent people.'"[17] This stream's main contribution to the larger missional movement (besides paving the way for it in North America) is the commitment to keep theology and practice, as well as church and mission, integrally together.

The mosaic stream, with its emphasis upon the need for the church to reflect the diversity that is humanity, stresses the truth that the flow of mission is no longer (if it ever was) West to East, North to South, and white to non-white.[18] Rather, mission is the call upon the whole church, in all its gender, cultural, and class diversity, to proclaim the whole gospel to the whole world. Those who swim here—mostly those among African-, Hispanic-, Asian-, and Native-American Christians who see white dominance and privilege losing ground—work toward justice, cultural diversity, and racial reconciliation as nonnegotiable tasks of kingdom mission. "What does evangelism have to do with social justice and racial and ethnic reconciliation?" asks Brenda Salter McNeil. "Everything," she answers, "if we take Jesus seriously."[19] The commitment to contextualization, racial equality and justice, and the formation of multicultural churches is an indispensable contribution of this stream to the larger missional movement.

Finally, the monastic stream, with its emphasis upon radical simplicity, community, and selfless service (especially with and for the most vulnerable in society), stresses the importance of the church as an alternative community that challenges consumerism, cultural accommodation, and apathy. Those who swim here—mostly young evangelicals who draw upon "the richness of the Catholic, Orthodox, Celt, and Anglican monastic traditions"[20]—profoundly challenge the caricature of contemplatives as people who don't care about the world. In *The New Friars,* Scott Bessenecker describes the young contemplatives as "burning with passion to serve the destitute in slum communities of the developing world—not from a position of power but from alongside them, living in the same makeshift housing, breathing the same sewage-tainted air, subject to the same government bulldozers that threaten to raze their communities."[21] The development of a spirituality of mission, as well as the demonstration that it is not impossible to live out the radical dimensions of the gospel, have profoundly shaped today's missional church movement.

To be missional, therefore, means *to join God's mission to transform the world, as the church strives in the Spirit to be authentically relational, intellectually and theologically grounded, culturally and socio-economically diverse, and radically committed to both God and neighbor, especially the poor.*

The question that presents itself to us as preachers and teachers is this: If we take this understanding seriously, if we decide to look through missional lenses when we read, study, and interpret the Scriptures, irrespective of which stream we swim in, how would it inform and change our preaching?

In addressing this question, this book is divided into two main parts. I contend that certain convictions must inform the mind and heart of the missional preacher. Part 1 of this book lays these out—three essentials, to be exact—that need to be in operation if missional preaching is to occur. Part 2 builds upon these essentials as it discusses seven goals that spell out what this type of gospel communication hopes to accomplish. Each of the seven chapters in Part 2 is followed by a sample sermon that illustrates what missional preaching looks like.

Between the essentials and the goals of missional preaching described in this book, readers will encounter a broad range of topics—very broad! There is much to absorb in these pages. Tackling something as big as God's mission in the world lends itself to this. But this book is also intentionally broad, wanting to give readers more of an overview of what it takes to preach missionally rather than to go in-depth with any one of these topics. Indeed whole books could be (and have been) written for each of these topics. I will leave it to others to go deeper with any or all of these, as the Spirit moves them.

NOTES

1. A line from the Beatles's classic hit, "Eleanor Rigby," *Revolver* (1966).
2. Lesslie Newbigin, *The Open Secret* (Grand Rapids: Eerdmans, 1995), 30–34; David J. Bosch, *Transforming Mission* (Maryknoll, NY: Orbis, 1991), 15–24; Arthur Glasser, *Announcing the Kingdom* (Grand Rapids: Baker Academic, 2003), 17; Christopher J. H. Wright, *The Mission of God* (Downers Grove: IVP, 2007), 22.
3. Darrell Guder et al., *Missional Church: A Vision for the Sending of the Church in North America* (Grand Rapids: Eerdmans, 1998), 3.
4. Guder, *Missional Church*, 3.
5. Eunjoo Mary Kim, "The Missionary God and Missionary Preaching," unpublished manuscript (Iliff School of Theology, Denver, 2007), 2. See also Newbigin, *The Open Secret*, 29.
6. Kim, "The Missionary God and Missionary Preaching," 3.
7. Leo Tolstoy, *What Men Live By* (White Plains: Peter Pauper Press, 1965), 58.
8. Emil Brunner, *The Word and the World,* reprinted edition (Lexington, KY: American Theological Library Association, 1965), 108.
9. Guder, *Missional Church,* 135.
10. Guder, *Missional Church,* 135.
11. Doug Pagitt, *Preaching Re-Imagined* (Grand Rapids: Zondervan, 2005), 23–24. According to Pagitt, "progressional dialogue" is "where the content of the presentation is established in the context of a healthy relationship between the presenter and the listeners, and substantive changes in the content are then created as a result of this relationship."
12. John A. Dally, *Choosing the Kingdom: Missional Preaching for the Household of God* (Herndon, VA: Alban, 2008), 5.
13. Lois Y. Barrett et al., *Treasure in Clay Jars: Patterns in Missional Faithfulness* (Grand Rapids: Eerdmans, 2004), 159–161.
14. Darrell Guder, quoted in Tom Sine, *The New Conspirators* (Downers Grove: IVP, 2008), 43.
15. Barrett, *Treasure in Clay Jars*, xi.
16. Tom Sine, *The New Conspirators* (Downers Grove: IVP, 2008), 31–55.
17. Sine, *The New Conspirators*, 41.
18. This is the thesis of Philip Jenkins's *The Next Christendom* (New York: Oxford University, 2002). For a treatment of this shift specifically in the evangelical church in the United States, see Soong Chan Rah, *The Next Evangelicalism* (Downers Grove: IVP, 2009).
19. Brenda Salter McNeil, *A Credible Witness* (Downers Grove: IVP, 2008), 18.
20. Sine, *The New Conspirators,* 49.
21. Scott A. Bessenecker, *The New Friars* (Downers Grove: IVP, 2006), 16.

PART 1

The Essentials
of Missional Preaching

When our lives and words line up—when, in a word, integrity exists—preaching can be a powerful thing. The opposite also rings true: When preachers teach others not to judge but have a judgmental spirit, or when they teach against gossip but are known to be gossips, then preaching is dismissible, laughable, and even detrimental to the cause of the gospel. This is Homiletics 101 (and, for that matter, Christian Life 101).

In this light, missional preaching derives its power when the communicator herself is possessed by God and God's purposes, when she models a life committed to bearing witness to the gospel in the world. If we have not submitted wholly to the God of mission with our heads, hearts, and hands, then it would be difficult to be convincing. But when we begin to internalize God's mission, when it becomes evident that mission has permeated our lives, then our words take on power. Only those who have become, or are becoming, truly missional can effectively pull off missional preaching.

At least three essentials, which are respectively theological, biblical, and liturgical in nature, define preachers who have been possessed by the God of mission. First, we need to have a clear and firm grasp of the idea of the *missio Dei*, a biblical reality that theologically grounds mission in the person of God. Second, we must read the

Bible missionally; that is, we need to see mission as the interpretive framework within which all of Scripture derives its meaning. And third, we need to commit to keeping the integral relationship between worship and mission liturgically intact. To the extent that we incorporate these three essentials in our sermon craft, the possibility of missional preaching is within range.

CHAPTER 1

MISSIO DEI:
The Mission of God Needs a Church

Of the three essentials of missional preaching, the theological no-tion of the *missio Dei* takes precedence. Like the word *missional*, the phrase *missio Dei* has enjoyed quite a burst of popularity in recent years; if one "Googles" it, for example, the results would yield more than seventy thousand hits. In a relatively short span of time, count-less theologians (armchair and professional alike) have filled the blo-gosphere with thoughts about *missio Dei*, a plethora of articles and books have been written on it, and churches have been named after it. It is indeed a part of the ethos of the missional movement. And just like *missional*, its definition, its history, and its implications have become somewhat murky. What exactly does this Latin phrase mean, and why is it so foundational to missional preaching?

A Very Theological Idea

Missio Dei refers to the idea that mission flows out from the very being of God. It refers to the nature of God as that which fundamen-tally justifies and motivates mission in the world—not the expansion of the church, the salvation of souls from eternal lostness, the weight of human need, and certainly not the spread of Western Christian culture upon the non-Western world. Except for the last one, these motivations are not so much wrong as they are limited in that they are pragmatically driven and human-based.

Against such motives, which have pervaded the missionary enterprise for centuries, the idea of a radically theological or theocentric source of mission began to surface in the early 1930s. The heart of this notion is that mission begins and ends not with human activity but with the activities of, in, and through the trinitarian Godhead. Most mission theologians credit Karl Barth for providing the impetus for the idea of the *missio Dei,* particularly in his theology of God's self-revelation, actions, and reconciliation.[1] Barth did not, however, coin the term. It was a lesser-known "Karl," as in theologian Karl Hartenstein at the International Missionary Council meeting in Willingen, Germany, in 1952 who is believed to be the first to utilize the term for mission.[2] Then, in 1965, George Vicedom published a book entitled *The Mission of God,* which was the first attempt to develop the idea fully.[3]

Renowned missiologist David J. Bosch articulates the *missio Dei* concisely when he writes: "Mission is, primarily and ultimately, the work of the Triune God, Creator, Redeemer, and Sanctifier, for the sake of the world. . . . Mission has its origin in the heart of God. God is a fountain of sending love. This is the deepest source of mission. It is impossible to penetrate deeper still; there is mission because God loves people."[4] Bosch goes on to claim that "since Willingen, the understanding of mission as *missio Dei* has been embraced by virtually all Christian persuasions."[5] Mission theologians including Lesslie Newbigin, H. H. Rosin, Anastasios of Androusa, Orlando Costas, Andrew Kirk, and the core leaders of the Gospel in Our Culture Network have all done their part to develop this theological understanding for mission since Willingen.

Several features of *missio Dei* are important to point out, albeit briefly, in order to gain a fuller understanding of the profoundly theological root of mission.

Mission Is God Sending God

The *missio Dei* literally means "the sending of God."[6] Before the church was sent to engage in mission, God the Father sent God the Son (John 3:16-17). "As you have sent me into the world," Jesus prayed in John 17:18, "so I have sent them into the world." The order of his prayer defines the heart of the *missio Dei.* As Guder and colleagues assert, "Mission is the result of *God's* initiative, rooted in *God's* purposes to restore and heal creation."[7]

Moreover, the Father and the Son have sent the Holy Spirit in order to complete the work of redemption in creation (John 15:26; Acts 1:8). According to the mystery of God as Trinity, mission flows from the harmonious divine community of Father, Son, and Holy Spirit, sending or revealing God's self into the world in order to redeem it. The *missio Dei* is finally *missio Trinitatis.*[8]

This overtly New Testament understanding of trinitarian mission, however, does not mean that the *missio Dei* had no prior existence. On the contrary, God was in the business of sending or revealing God's self redemptively in the Old Testament, long before there was any clear theological articulation of the Trinity (which did not solidify into fundamental Christian doctrine until the fourth century).[9] The mission of God did not begin with the Father sending the Son; it began with God sending God-self to Abram, who was sent out to establish a great nation through which all the families of the earth would be blessed (Gen. 12:1-3). However, the theological articulation of the doctrine of the Trinity provides the clearest and strongest affirmation of mission as being rooted in the *intra*-active being of God. Indeed, God has been sending God-self into the world since the beginning of time.

Mission Is God's Gaze upon the World

If mission originates from God, then mission's spatial range can be nothing less than the whole world God created. The starting point for mission in this sense is nothing less than God's gaze upon the universe. The beginning of mission as God's desire to save creation in its entirety constitutes a second defining feature of *missio Dei.* Historically, the idea of *missio Dei* was proposed to counter the overly prominent place the church occupied for mission. Because of its inappropriately central role, "the church's missionary mandate lay not only in forming the church of Jesus Christ, but in shaping the Christian communities that it birthed in the image of the church of western European culture."[10] *Missio Dei* sought to replace ecclesiocentric and Eurocentric understandings of mission. It shifted the missional pattern from "church-God-world" to "God-world-church."[11]

Admittedly, this new pattern opened the door to gross misunderstandings, which took God's mission well beyond biblical parameters. In the hands of some, *missio Dei* expanded to mean that all roads lead to God and that God's ways with people are not bound by the gospel of Jesus Christ as traditional Christianity understood it.[12] Such theologies of mission minimized the role of the church and marginalized the place of evangelization in the mission of God.

Although God and God's mission are certainly not bound by the church, the idea of the *missio Dei* can lead to a universalistic free-for-all if we do not take into account the biblical truths that the church embodies. But if we take the Bible seriously, then God's mission, big as it is, places Jesus Christ of the Gospels at the very center of that mission. I will say more about the place of the church in the *missio Dei* shortly. The important idea to grasp here is that it is God's redemptive, loving gaze upon the whole world—and nothing less—that launches mission.

Mission Is God's Broad Agenda

Inseparable from God's universal eye is God's broad agenda, which further deepens the meaning of *missio Dei*. God loves creation in its entirety and longs to save it, but from what? In light of who God is—Creator, Sustainer, and Lover of the world—could God's missional agenda be anything less than everything? Is there anything God does not seek to save? The answer, of course, is no; God's agenda for saving all that is lost and broken is necessarily as big as the world. The effects of the Fall (Gen. 3) permeate everything—broken relationships all around between God, humanity, and creation. Since the Fall, human brokenness has manifested itself in violence, injustice, oppression, alienation, despair, disease, environmental abuse, and fractured relationships on all levels of existence—spiritual, social, political, familial, and psycho-emotional. And God's plan to redeem and make whole includes all these dimensions of existence.

In kingdom-of-God terms, which I will develop further in the next chapter, God's agenda has to do with reestablishing God's reign, God's *shalom*, upon every dimension of life. And where God fully reigns, peace, justice, righteousness, mercy, grace, and love also reign, resulting in reconciled relationships between God, humanity, and creation.

I am aware of the strong objection to such a broad missional perspective, namely the critique that says, "If everything is mission, then nothing is mission."[13] Some might argue that leading the church toward maturity in Christ constitutes an act of mission—and indeed God's agenda includes the health of the church. But the *mis-*

sio Dei certainly would be misconstrued if churches use it to justify a non-active, non-missional, maintenance posture that concerns itself with the church alone. The *missio Dei* goes beyond establishing righteousness, justice, peace, and love among the redeemed; God's mission seeks to establish these very realities for the whole world.

Mission Is God Sending the Church

Finally, the *missio Dei* involves the church. Only after we wrap our heads around mission as a core attribute of God's very being can we now consider the role of the church in that mission. The church, however, is more than an afterthought. "The classical doctrine of the *missio Dei* as God the Father sending the Son, and God the Father and God the Son sending the Spirit was expanded to include yet another movement: Father, Son and Holy Spirit sending the church into the world."[14]

The *missio Dei* carries with it the idea that God has chosen to work primarily through those whom God has redeemed in order to establish God's reign on earth. From the formation of Israel in the Old Testament to the Jewish-Gentile churches in the New, it is clear that God's strategy involves forming and mobilizing a community of people—imperfect as they (and we) are—to accomplish the divine plan. As the motto of the Center for Parish Development asserts, "God has a mission . . . and God's mission needs a church."[15]

The idea of *missio Dei* gets distorted if the church is excluded or marginalized. When we fail to emphasize the centrality of the church's participation in God's activities in the world, we stray from the mission's biblical moorings. In such cases, the church can easily lose its motivation to engage in proactive mission—why should we, when God is already doing the work, to which we are neither privy nor invited? Furthermore, a distorted *missio Dei* can also render anemic the blood of Christ, the very power of the gospel to save— what's so special about Christ's blood spilled on our behalf if it is but one way of salvation among many? In a biblically framed *missio Dei*, however, the community of the cross and resurrection of Christ plays a vital role. If God is the lead actor, then the Spirit-empowered, Truth-bearing church of Jesus Christ makes up the indispensable supporting cast. I repeat: The church is not a mere afterthought. God has mandated the participation of God's people in God's mission to transform the world.

The church, however, is more than just an instrument to be used to accomplish God's agenda, as if God has simply hired a group of people to work in the harvest fields. The church itself also reflects the product of God's mission. Before we are missionaries, we are God's children. God invites us to enter into the kingdom and to enjoy abundant life, both personally and corporately as the church. I respectfully disagree with Guder and colleagues who say, "We have begun to see that the church of Jesus Christ is not the purpose or goal of the gospel, but rather its instruments and witness."[16] It is not either/or; the church is both the fruit of and the primary instrument for the work of the gospel. Even as the church enjoys God's salvation, it grows in its sense of cooperation with God to heal a broken world. The preacher's call to salvation, therefore, does not just consist of becoming born again in Christ, to use a familiar phrase, but also to be born again in Christ's community called the church and in Christ's purposes in and for the world. As James Choung writes, "We need a gospel that incorporates our personal transformation, our need for community, and our call to love our neighbors in the world."[17]

Preaching the *Missio Dei*

The Center for Parish Development has it right: "God has a mission, and God's mission needs a church." And I doubt anyone would argue if I were to add, ". . . and the church needs preachers who understand that God has a mission." The *missio Dei* underscores the missional nature of God, and as we internalize this truth, several important principles should guide and shape our preaching.

It's All about God

First, because of the *missio Dei,* we preach the centrality of God in all things. Church and humanity are not the center of the universe; God is. All of life revolves around God and God's desires for the world. The mission of the church, therefore, has meaning only as it is grounded in the missional being of God. "The most crucial issue in missions," John Piper asserts, "is the centrality of God in the life of the church."[18] As such, whatever we call the church to do in our preaching should point to the sovereignty and centrality of Father, Son, and Holy Spirit. God seeks to save God's world through God's people. Mission is derived from, driven by, and points to God. The *missio Dei* loudly declares that, from beginning to end, it's all about God!

Being the Church as Mission

Second, because of the *missio Dei*, we preach that everything we do to build up the church is part of God's mission. As I mentioned earlier, the church is both the fruit and the instrument of God's redemptive activities. As such, the church, just by virtue of *being* the church, bears witness to life in the kingdom for all to see and experience. Referring to ancient Israel, Ronald J. Sider and colleagues write, "God's covenantal call to the newly formed people to model his reign reflected what God desired for the whole world."[19] The same call rests upon God's people today—namely, to demonstrate peace in the midst of war, justice in the midst of injustice, and love in the midst of hatred and alienation, all in and through the community life of the church. Simply *being* the church provides an alternative to a broken world. In this light we preach that the church itself is mission.

Perhaps better than any other tradition, the Eastern Orthodox Church has kept the sacramental, missional nature of the church itself in the consciousness of the larger Body of Christ. In one of its definitive missionary statements, it says, "The church, the people of God in the communion of the Holy Spirit, is missionary in its very being, ever proceeding and ever gathering, pulsating with God's all-embracing love and unity. The church, as the presence of the kingdom of God in the world, illuminates in one single reality the glory of God and the eschatological destiny of creation."[20]

The more mature and healthy and loving the people of God become with one another, the greater is the church's witness in the world (John 13:35). We preach, therefore, that even the in-house activities of the church, insofar as they build-up the community of Christ, are missional in nature. From Sunday worship to committee meetings to prayer vigils to counseling sessions to choir rehearsals to small groups to potlucks—these activities contribute to the mission of God, insomuch as they contribute to the overall health of the alternative community. We preach toward a healthy church, which in and of itself shines God's light upon the world.

The Mission-hood of All Believers

Finally, because of the *missio Dei*, we preach that all God's children have a part to play in accomplishing God's purposes. I affirm the adage, "Everyone is a missionary"—but not in the sense that all should knock on doors and distribute tracts. Rather, I believe all

Christians should view their respective spiritual gifts as both for the edification of the church and the transformation of the world. As God's people sit under the teaching of a missional pastor, they begin to see the missional value of the spiritual gifts that different individuals possess, whether it be mercy, hospitality, service, administration, prophecy, evangelism, or other gifts.

In light of the *missio Dei*, we preach that bearing witness comes in many forms. Yes, there is verbal proclamation for those gifted in evangelism, but there is also opening one's home to the needy for those gifted in hospitality, visiting the prisoner for those gifted in mercy, organizing a peace rally for those gifted in prophecy and administration, tutoring at-risk, academically challenged children for those gifted in compassion and teaching, and so on. In the hands of God, all these activities form into a beautiful and powerful witness to the kingdom of God. This type of preaching liberates God's people to actions that correspond with the gifts God has given each of them. The *missio Dei* prevents relegating mission to specialists; the call to missional engagement is upon the whole church in all its Spirit-breathed giftedness. Not everyone is an evangelist or a full-time professional missionary, but all are called and equipped to take part in God's mission.

The *missio Dei* maintains the supremacy of God in all things, calls the church to *be* the church as a form of witness to an alternative reality, and equips God's people to use their gifts for the transformation of the world. Missional preaching begins here.

NOTES

1. Karl Barth, *God in Action* (Manhasset, NY: Round Table Press, 1963). See also Waldron Scott, *Karl Barth's Theology of Mission* (Downers Grove: IVP, 1978).

2. Lalsangkima Pachuau, "Missio Dei," in *Dictionary of Mission Theology: Evangelical Foundations*, ed. John Corrie (Downers Grove: IVP, 2007), 233. Even though Hartenstein brought the term *"missio Dei"* to the fore in 1952 at Willingen, he actually coined it in 1933 in his book, *Die Mission als theologisches Problem: Beitrage zum grundsatzlichen Versandnis der Mission* (Berlin, Germany: Furch, 1933).

3. George Vicedom, *The Mission of God: An Introduction to a Theology of Mission* (St. Louis: Concordia, 1965).

4. David J. Bosch, *Transforming Mission* (Maryknoll, NY: Orbis, 1991), 390.

5. Bosch, *Transforming Mission,* 390.

6. John A. McIntosh, "Missio Dei," in *Evangelical Dictionary of World Missions,* ed. A. Scott Moreau (Grand Rapids: Baker, 2000), 631.

7. Darrel Guder et al., *Missional Church: A Vision for Sending of the Church in North America* (Grand Rapids: Eerdmans, 1998), 4. Emphasis added.

8. J. Andrew Kirk, *What is Mission? Theological Explorations* (Minneapolis: Fortress, 2000), 27.

9. Stanley J. Grenz, *Theology for the Community of God* (Grand Rapids: Eerdmans, 2000), 53–65.

10. Guder et al., *Missional Church,* 4.

11. Theologian Johannes C. Hoekenndijk arguably did the most to make this shift happen with his insistence that the arena of God's activities was the arena of human affairs, not the church. See McIntosh, "Missio Dei," 632–33, for a concise treatment of Hoekendijk's role in the development of *missio Dei.*

12. Tormond Engelsviken, "*Missio Dei:* The Understanding and Misunderstanding of a Theological Concept in European Churches and Missiology," *International Review of Mission* XCII (367), 486–490. See also James A. Scherer, "Church, Kingdom and *Missio Dei,*" in *The Good News of the Kingdom: Mission Theology for the Third Millennium,* eds. Charles Van Engen, Dean S. Gilliland, and Paul Pierson (Maryknoll, NY: Orbis, 1993), 85–86.

13. Stephen C. Neill, *Creative Tension* (London: Edinburgh House, 1959), 81.

14. Bosch, *Transforming Mission,* 390.

15. The Center for Parish Development, http://www.missionalchurch.org/pages/gods_mission_wkshp.html (accessed January 15, 2009).

16. Guder et al, *Missional Church,* 5.

17. James Choung, *True Story: A Christianity Worth Believing In* (Downers Grove: IVP, 2008), 12.

18. John Piper, *Let the Nations Be Glad! The Supremacy of God in Missions* (Grand Rapids: Baker, 1993), 14.

19. Ronald J. Sider, John M. Perkins, Wayne L. Gordon, and F. Albert Tizon, *Linking Arms, Linking Lives: How Urban-Suburban Partnerships Can Transform Communities* (Grand Rapids: Baker, 2008), 44.

20. "Final Report of CWME Consultation of Eastern Orthodox and Oriental Orthodox Churches," in *New Directions in Mission & Evangelization 1,* eds. James A. Scherer and Stephen B. Bevans (Maryknoll, NY: Orbis, 1992), 236.

CHAPTER 2

KINGDOM HERMENEUTICS: The Missional Basis of the Bible

I belong to the Evangelical Covenant Church, a small but growing denomination essentially founded on the simple question of the old Pietists, "Where is it written?" Of course, this speaks to the notion that whatever Covenanters have believed and affirmed throughout their 120 years of existence must be found in the pages of Scripture.[1] My denomination is certainly not alone in affirming the centrality of the Bible in matters of faith and practice, nor is this commitment unique to churches in the evangelical Protestant tradition. Indeed, although their approaches to Scripture may differ (sometimes wildly so!), all Christian traditions seek some level of biblical justification for their convictions, doctrines, and practices.

Given this reality, allow me to state the obvious: Our preaching in and for the church must be biblical. The Bible is what in fact distinguishes a sermon from other forms of public speaking. A speech from the President of the United States, for example, may be eloquent, passionate, and even spiritual; it might even include quotes from Scripture. But because the Bible does not serve as the framework and foundation for political speeches (nor should it), they are not sermons. A sermon is an exposition of a *biblical* passage, a *biblical* story, and/or a *biblical* principle for the edification of the church, the transformation of the world, and the glory of God. A sermon should certainly reflect and speak to the current context and time, but it interprets the events of today from a biblical perspective. Much of what passes for preaching misses the mark precisely because the Bible does not serve as its primary basis. If we ministers would genuinely practice our fundamental call as preachers (and not just as public speakers), we must be expositors, interpreters, and teachers of Scripture, even as we do the hard work of negotiating the relationship between text and context.

Toward a Missional Hermeneutic

In my view, if a pastor engages in preaching that is truly biblical—which I have asserted is the only true kind of preaching—she also engages in preaching that is missional. Biblical preaching is missional preaching. This lies at the heart of the second essential. The Bible must be seen as wholly and thoroughly missional. Missional preachers understand that the Bible does not just provide specific texts to formulate an understanding of mission; on the contrary, we affirm with missiologist Arthur Glasser that, "the whole Bible, both Old and New Testaments, is a missionary book, the revelation of God's purpose and action in mission in human history."[2]

Old Testament scholar Christopher J. H. Wright takes it a step further and contends that the Bible does not so much provide the basis for mission as mission has provided the basis for the Bible—meaning, that the Bible testifies to God's prior redemptive activity in the world.[3] He writes, "The writings that now comprise our Bible are themselves the product of and witness to the ultimate mission of God."[4] I read this as saying, among other things, that God's saving acts came first; the complex, human-and-divine processes that produced what we now call the Bible bears witness to them. In this light Wright's project seeks not to find biblical support for mission, but to develop a missional hermeneutic with which to understand the whole of Scripture. He explains:

> Many others have produced fine and comprehensive works establishing a biblical foundation for mission. My major concern has been to develop an approach to biblical hermeneutics that sees the mission of God as a framework within which we can read the whole Bible. Mission is, in my view, a major key that unlocks the whole grand narrative of the canon of Scripture.[5]

Preaching that seeks to be missional requires this kind of approach to the Bible. It requires seeing God's missional heart and corresponding actions as the guiding theme from Genesis to Revelation. Seeing only selected passages as missionary in nature—the book of Jonah, Matthew 28:18-20, and Acts 1:8, to name a few favorites—will not do. As we develop missional eyes, the Genesis story of creation reads like the vision of *shalom* that it is—God, people, and creation in right relationship with one another. Moses and Esther become models of those who forsook their respective places of privilege and chose instead to stand in solidarity with the oppressed. The Proverbs become wisdom for a life committed to God and God's purposes. The prophets come alive with their message of God's judgment against injustice and idolatry, as well as God's relentless love that seeks to transform Israel and the world. Jesus becomes not just the crux of salvation history, but the ultimate missionary who leaves the comforts of heaven in order to dwell among us for our salvation. The Holy Spirit becomes the presence of God, empowering the church to bear witness to the gospel in Jerusalem, in all Judea and Samaria, and to the ends of the earth. The letters of Paul read as responses to situations of churches engaged in body life and mission. And the battle of the cosmos in the book of Revelation vividly portrays the victory of God over Satan and the evils of idolatry, injustice, and poverty. The whole Bible comes alive and becomes, in its totality, not only the record of God's redemptive activity in the past but also the impetus for the church's participation in God's mission now and in the future.

I am aware of the critical biblical scholarship that has rightfully asserted the many different historical, cultural, traditional, literary, and personal perspectives contained in the Scriptures themselves.[6] For some, to employ a single theme in an effort to unify the Bible is to impose the modern interpreter's bias upon what is otherwise a collection of diverse and disparate narratives. For others, the divinely inspired formation of the Bible—not just the writing of the books, but also the acceptance and organization of the books into an authoritative canon—gave theological shape to the Book and provides a certain level of unity. Is there is a single, overarching biblical theology, or is it more accurate to view the Bible as containing many theologies? To go on about the issue of the unity and diversity of Scripture (the domain of the discipline of biblical theology) would lead us hope-lessly astray.[7] Suffice it to say that unity and diversity in the Bible are not mutually exclusive; that the various perspectives within Scripture form what Vern Poythress calls a "symphonic theology"—a sonic, cohesive, and profoundly moving unity that acknowledges the con-tribution of each and every instrument.[8] I argue that the symphonic theology of the Bible is ultimately the music of mission.

Granted that I am a missiologist; so if I err, I err on the side of see-ing mission everywhere. It is true that we all bring our biases to the text, but does not the Bible itself invite a missional reading? Wright argues compellingly that the books of both the Old and New Testa-ments were written in response to missionary situations. Regarding the New Testament books, Wright quotes Howard Marshall as say-ing, "It may be more helpful to recognize them more specifically as the documents of a mission."[9] And as for the Old Testament books, "we can see that many of these texts emerged out of the engagement of Israel with the surrounding world. . . . People produced texts in re-lation to what they believed God had done, was doing or would do in their world."[10] The pages of Scripture offer God's people in every age a moving, compelling, and urgent call to engage in God's mission.

Bible, Kingdom, and Mission

One of Poythress's twelve maxims of symphonic theology states that any of the themes or motifs found in Scripture can serve as a valid lens through which the whole Bible can be understood.[11] I agree; however, I see one biblical theme as "more equal than others"— namely, the overarching reality of the reign or kingdom of God. Few would argue with the notion that the kingdom of God was central to the life, teachings, and overall mission of Jesus.[12] It stands to reason that if the kingdom of God is central to Jesus, then it should be cen-tral to the church of Jesus.

The kingdom theme, however, goes further back than the Gospels; indeed, it can be traced back to creation. Theologian Ken Gnanakan writes, "Theologies of mission that only start with the New Testa-ment lack the firm and full foundation of God's mission as it has been gradually revealed from creation. . . . Our theology of mission asserts that God has a plan for his world with ultimate dimensions that re-late to his kingdom."[13] In the classic book *The Kingdom of God*, distinguished Old Testament scholar John Bright claims that the theme of the kingdom of God "is found in one form or another through the length and breadth of the Bible."[14] So when Jesus announced that the kingdom of God was at hand (Mark 1:14-15), his Jewish audience knew what he was talking about. Wishfully, Bright writes that if he were given the opportunity to give a title to the Bible, he would call it, "The Book of the Coming Kingdom of God."[15]

The kingdom refers to a reality that is characterized by God's rule, reflected most profoundly, powerfully, and completely in Jesus Christ. To the extent that God in Christ rules, reconciliation between God and people, between people and people, and between God, people, and creation happens. To the extent that God in Christ rules, righteousness, peace, mercy, justice, and love shape reality, from the domain of the human heart to the sociopolitical structures of nations to the order of the cosmos.

It is this biblical kingdom that serves as the basis of the mission of Jesus—and, therefore, of the church. Numerous theologians and missiologists have pointed this out. Mission professor Mortimer Arias, for example, reminds the church that the gospel to which it testifies is the gospel of the kingdom.[16] Ethicist Murray Dempster makes a case that the basis of both evangelism and social concern is the kingdom of God.[17] The theologians who drafted the "Kingdom Manifesto on the Whole Gospel" and "Kingdom Affirmations and Commitments"—the result of a series of consultations that brought together evangelists, social activists, and charismatic renewal advocates—make it clear that the three missionary streams of evangelism, social justice, and signs and wonders flow from the river of the kingdom of God.[18] Moreover, official Catholic, Orthodox, mainline, and evangelical Protestant mission statements all make the kingdom of God central to their understandings of the church's mission.[19]

At the risk of oversimplification, I found the following broad outline to be helpful in viewing the whole of Scripture in terms of the kingdom of God:

1. God's Rule in Creation and Fall (Genesis 1–11)

2. God's Rule in Israel (Genesis 12—Esther)

3. God's Rule through the Sages and Prophets (Job—Malachi)

4. God's Rule in Christ (Matthew—John)

5. God's Rule through a Spirit-Empowered Church (Acts—Jude)

6. God's Rule in the New Heaven and New Earth (Revelation)

Of course, this simple framing represents not *the* way, but *a* way to organize Scripture that enables us to interpret the Bible's events, stories, and teachings through a kingdom grid.[20] So in God's Rule in Creation and Fall, the goodness of creation is precisely because God ruled the earth, and the mar of creation occurred because humankind succumbed to the lure of becoming ruler-gods themselves. In God's Rule in Israel, we can interpret the Abrahamic, Mosaic, and Davidic covenants as God's initiatives to restore God's rule via a particular people—namely, the Hebrews-turned-nation-of-Israel—for the sake of all peoples. The idea was that through the formation of a people of God, which would live out the divine ethics of peace, mercy, justice, and righteousness on both the personal and sociopolitical levels, all the peoples of the earth would have the opportunity to see what life would be like if Yahweh God ruled.

The call upon the people of God to live in obedience to God's reign proved to be impossible for Israel. From early grumblings right after the miraculous exodus to the unstable period of the judges to the tragic events of the monarchy, God's people failed to stay faithful to the one true God and to uphold justice. In God's Rule through the Sages and Prophets, we can interpret the songs, laments, and prophecies in Israel as keeping the notion of the kingdom of God alive in the hearts and minds of the people, despite the failures of the nation. As the sages kept them singing and reflecting deeply on true spirituality, the prophets pointed to the promise of the coming kingdom via a messiah in the line of David, even as they pronounced judgment upon Israel's unfaithfulness and injustice.

The four Gospels record the arrival of the long-expected messiah in the person of Jesus Christ. God's Rule in Christ is the crux of the kingdom story, as the birth, life, teaching, death, and resurrection of Christ inaugurate the fulfillment of the hope of the kingdom. Israel's missional call was to embody the kingdom in its national life; Jesus embodied it in his person. Jesus was the kingdom of God incarnate, as he ministered compassion, justice, and forgiveness by word, deed, and miraculous signs, and as he taught the truths and values of the kingdom in ways accessible to the masses. As we know, the forces of darkness tried to snuff the kingdom out by killing Jesus; but death had no ultimate power, as Christ rose on the third day. As long as Jesus is alive, the kingdom is here!

On the strength of the kingdom's presence, the missional call to proclaim the good news of the kingdom was passed on to Christ's followers. In God's Rule through a Spirit-Empowered Church, the disciples were not left as orphans, as the very real presence of the Holy Spirit strengthened and emboldened them. By the power and direction of the Spirit, these disciples not only embodied the kingdom in a multiethnic community in which Jews and Gentiles came together (a profound picture of the kingdom in and of itself), but also extended the message and values of the kingdom to all people and creation. Insofar as these categories represent periods of time, **WE ARE HERE.** The Spirit-empowered church today continues to advance God's rule in its life, deeds, and words.

Finally, in God's Rule in the New Heaven and New Earth, we get a glimpse of the future of God, when the cosmic struggle between good and evil comes to an end, and Jesus will reign as *Cristus Victor.* Jesus will take his rightful place as Lord of lords and King of kings—designations that are often used as metaphors today, but will be literal in the future! The struggles that plague creation will end, and the kingdom of God will prevail.

Kingdom-Shaped Preaching

As we are nourished by the missional richness of God's Word from Genesis to Revelation, we as preachers begin to serve a healthy diet to the church, refueling it for holy action. Instead of serving "the baked potatoes of love, the melting butter of grace, with just enough bacon and chives of outreach to ease the conscience"[21]—all of which sedate God's people—preachers who have feasted upon the rich biblical story of the kingdom of God end up feeding the flock with the essential vitamins and minerals for authentic missional life. A number of guiding principles for preaching emerge when our hermeneutical lenses are in the shape of the kingdom of God.

Big Mission

First, because of the biblical kingdom, we preach in light of the big picture of God's ultimate desire for the world. God's project of peace, justice, reconciliation, righteousness, and love for all—in a word, *shalom*—is massive. "The gospel [of the kingdom]," Michael Goheen and Craig Bartholomew claim, "is an announcement about where God is moving the history of the whole world."[22] But the all-embracing scope of God's big mission too easily gets lost like the proverbial forest amid the trees of everyday life and ministry. Preaching that is informed by the biblical kingdom, however, keeps the universal nature of God's purposes in view, maintaining its place as the source of all the church is and does. In light of the kingdom of God nothing that the church does is meaningless or mundane as it contributes to the big mission of God. We need to encourage our flocks with this truth on a regular basis.

For All Peoples through a People

This leads to the second guiding preaching principle that is informed by the biblical kingdom—namely, that we preach the importance of community. From the call to Abraham and Sarah to the birth of the nation of Israel to the development of the Christ-centered, Spirit-empowered church, the biblical kingdom has revealed a God who forms a people in order to reach *all* peoples. This highlights, first of all, the importance of a unity among believers as a community whose main common denominator is faith in Christ. As such, the walls that divide women and men, black, white, and brown, young and old, rich and poor, and all other human-made divisions do not apply to the people of God (Gal. 3:28; Eph. 2:14). John Armstrong reminds us that the New Testament describes a church that "welcomed everyone—regardless of social status, ethnicity, gender, or wealth—into a family in which relationships were founded on a common Savior and unity was formed out of diversity."[23]

Furthermore, missional preaching not only highlights community, it also highlights the centrifugal nature of that community, sharing the overflowing blessings of life under the reign of God and inviting any and all to join the timeless, global, kingdom community. In other words it affirms the inseparability of church and mission. Kingdom-shaped, missional preaching does its indispensable part in molding the people of God to be the city on the hill, the salt of the earth, and the light of the world (Matt. 5:13-14).

Big Love

Third, because of the biblical kingdom, we preach the loving lordship of God in Christ. God's project to redeem the world is motivated by nothing than less than God's love for creation and everyone in it. The church may be somewhat anesthetized to the message of God's love in the face of the God-loves-you, bumper-sticker theologies that permeate much of what passes for evangelism today. As Armstrong asks, "Are we so comfortable with the idea that God loves us that this great mystery no longer moves us?"[24] In fact, the notion of a deity who relates to creation in covenantal love is as radical today as it was in ancient times. Power, authority, fear, law, obedience, distance, and inaccessibility readily come to mind when people think of the creator and sustainer of all existence—but love?

The biblical story of the kingdom of God is ultimately a love story. As New Testament scholar N. T. Wright asserts, "The story speaks from first to last of a God who did not need to create, but who did so out of overflowing and generous love. It speaks of a God who did not need to redeem and recreate, but did so as the greatest possible act of self-giving love."[25] The covenants recorded in Scripture define how this love was expressed historically, beginning with God's covenant with Noah and creation (Gen. 9:8-17), Abraham and Sarah (Gen. 15:1-6; 17:1-22), Moses and the nation of Israel (Ex. 19:1-8), and David and the kingdom of Israel (1 Sam. 13:13-14; 16:8-13). But of course, the New Covenant in Christ has given the fullest expression of God's love for the world (John 3:16), particularly in Jesus' death and resurrection.

Jesus is the crucified and risen king, but he is also our friend (John 15:9-17). As his followers, we are children of God, who have the privilege by the Holy Spirit to call God "*Abba*, Father" (Rom. 8:15; Gal. 4:6). By this love, which we ourselves have experienced, we go out into the world, with the cross and empty tomb as the enduring symbols of radical, kingdom love. As development practitioner and missiologist Bryant Myers asserts, "Any work of human transformation that does not announce this incredibly good news is fatally impoverished. The cross and resurrection are the very best news that we have."[26] So when our preaching flows from the biblical kingdom, we preach God's amazing love, experienced most fully in the person of Jesus Christ.

Missional Presence of the Future

Fourth, because of the biblical kingdom, we preach the future victory of God in Christ, as well as the present mission of the church in light of that victory. We preach the now-and-not-yet nature of the kingdom.[27] The not-yet part describes the divine sovereignty aspect of the kingdom; it is God who initiated the kingdom project, and God will bring it to fruition. The end of the biblical story promises the ultimate triumph of God, as the Revelator declares, "[God] will dwell with them as their God; they will be his peoples, and God himself will be with them; he will wipe every tear from their eyes. Death will be no more; mourning and crying and pain will be no more, for the first things have passed away" (Rev. 21:3-4). This future constitutes the hope of the Christian, of the church, and indeed, of the whole world. This future must inform our preaching, for what is our proclamation if it is not filled with hope? Our preaching, as homiletics professor Gennifer Brooks admonishes, must be "*good* news preaching," that is, "proclamation . . . of the good news of Jesus Christ as Savior of the world."[28] And this preaching, she continues, does not just rely on past events, but is "descriptive and representative of present reality and future promise . . . based on the substance of God's eternal, covenantal love for humanity as revealed in scripture."[29]

Missional preaching is hope-filled. God's people can count on this hope, "for these words are trustworthy and true" (Rev. 21:5). This certainty in God's future determines the church's mission. Theologian Chris Sugden puts it this way, "We start with the future to develop vision for the present."[30] This notion of the "presence of the future" is the "now" aspect of the now-and-not-yet kingdom, emphasizing human participation in God's mission. The kingdom is a gift to be enjoyed to the fullest in the future; but today, God calls upon the church to serve as signposts of the peace, justice, reconciliation, and righteousness to come in Jesus Christ. This is the mission of the people of hope who live in between the now and the not-yet.[31] Kingdom preaching, therefore, offers real hope, as well as inspires mission in light of that hope.

The biblical kingdom yields a rich harvest of significant themes: (1) the big picture of God's desire for the world; (2) the importance of community and the community's outward gaze; (3) the ultimate motivation of love; and (4) the reality and practice of hope. These biblical, kingdom themes inform and guide the art of missional sermon-craft. Without them, our pulpits are destined for insularity, emptiness, and mediocrity. Biblical preaching is kingdom preaching is missional preaching, and quite literally, the church's life depends on it.

NOTES

1. I am an ordained minister of the Evangelical Covenant Church. To see the place of the Bible in the ECC, see "Covenant Affirmations" at http://covchurch.org/uploads/cs/9S/cs9SiXBk7V9QsYP103JceQ/Covenant-AffirmationsBooklet.pdf (accessed 6 July 2010).
2. Arthur F. Glasser, *Announcing the Kingdom* (Grand Rapids: Baker, 2003), 17.
3. Christopher J. H. Wright, *The Mission of God* (Downers Grove: IVP, 2006), 29–69.
4. Wright, *Mission of God*, 22, 48.
5. Wright, *Mission of God*, 17.
6. See for example, *The Many Voices of the Bible*, eds. Sean Freyne and Ellen van Wolde (London, UK: SCM, 2002).
7. For a concise understanding of this issue, see *The Oxford Handbook of Biblical Studies*, eds. J.W. Rogerson and Judith M. Lieu (Oxford, UK: Oxford University, 2006), 675–774. The first three chapters of Part VI of this work, "The Interpretation of the Bible," are particularly helpful: Walter Breuggemann's "Old Testament Theology" (675–97), James Dunn's "New Testament Theology" (698–715), and Brend Janowski's "Biblical Theology" (716–31).
8. Vern Poythress, *Symphonic Theology: The Validity of Multiple Perspectives in Theology* (Grand Rapids: Zondervan, 1987).
9. I. Howard Marshall, in Wright, *The Mission of God*, 50.
10. Wright, *The Mission of God*, 50.
11. Poythress, *Symphonic Theology*, 86–87.
12. John Bright, *The Kingdom of God* (Nashville: Abingdon, 1953), 17ff. See also Donald Senior and Carroll Stuhlmueller, *The Biblical Foundations for Mission* (Maryknoll, NY: Orbis, 1983), 144.
13. Ken Gnanakan, *Kingdom Concerns: A Biblical Exploration toward a Theology of Mission* (Bangalore, India: Theological Book Trust, 1993), 45.
14. Bright, *The Kingdom of God*, 7.
15. Bright, *Kingdom of God*, 197.
16. Mortimer Arias, *Announcing the Reign of God: Evangelization and Subversive Memory of Jesus* (Minneapolis: Fortress, 1984), 1–12.
17. Murray W. Dempster, "Evangelism, Social Concern and the Kingdom of God," in *Called and Empowered*, eds. Murray W. Dempster, Byron D. Klaus, and Douglas Petersen (Boston: Hendrickson), 22–43. In the same volume, NT scholar Gordon Fee also makes a similar case in a chapter aptly entitled "The Kingdom of God and the Church's Global Mission" (7–21).
18. "Kingdom Manifesto on the Whole Gospel," and "Kingdom Affirmations and Commitments," *Transformation* 11/3 (July/September 1994), 1–7.
19. See *New Directions in Mission and Evangelization 1: Basic Statements 1974–1991*, eds. Stephen Bevans and James Scherer (Maryknoll, NY:

Orbis, 1992), where the editors have conveniently compiled important mission statements such as "Evangeli Nuntiandi" for Roman Catholics (91–98), "Go Forth in Peace" for Eastern Orthodox (203–31), "Ecumenical Affirmation: Mission and Evangelism" for Conciliar Protestants (36–51), and the "Lausanne Covenant" for Evangelical Protestants (253–59).

20. For other ways to see the missional unity of the Bible, see H. Dan Beeby, *Canon and Mission* (Harrisburg: Trinity Press Int'l, 1999), especially pp. 21–38.
21. Mark Labberton, *The Dangerous Act of Worship* (Downers Grove: IVP, 2007), 19.
22. Michael W. Goheen and Craig G. Bartholomew, *Living at the Crossroads: An Introduction to Christian Worldview* (Grand Rapids: Baker Academic, 2008), 2.
23. John H. Armstrong, *Your Church Is Too Small: Why Unity in Christ's Mission Is Vital to the Future of the Church* (Grand Rapids, MI: Zondervan, 2008), 47–48.
24. Armstrong, *Your Church is Too Small*, 47.
25. N. T. Wright, "The Bible for the Post Modern World," http://www.biblicaltheology.ca/blue_files/The%20Bible%20for%20the%20Post%20Modern%20World.pdf (accessed 21 June 2010).
26. Bryant Myers, *Walking with the Poor: Principles and Practices of Transformational Development* (Maryknoll, NY: Orbis, 1999), 37.
27. See Sze-kan Wan, "Kingdom of God," in *Global Dictionary of Theology*, eds. William A. Dyrness and Veli-Matti Karkkainen (Downers Grove, IL: IVP, 2008), 453–59, for a brief treatment of the nature of the kingdom from a global perspective.
28. Gennifer Brooks, *Good News Preaching: Offering the Gospel in Every Sermon* (Cleveland: The Pilgrim Press, 2009), 1. Emphasis added.
29. Brooks, *Good News Preaching*, 5.
30. Chris Sugden, "Transformational Development: Current State of Understanding and Practice," *Transformation* 20/2 (April 2003), 73.
31. See C. Rene Padilla, *Mission between the Times* Revised and Updated Edition (Guildford, UK: Langham Monographs, 2010). See also Al Tizon, *Transformation after Lausanne: Radical Evangelical Mission in Global-Local Perspective* (Oxford et. al.: Regnum and Eugene, OR: Wipf & Stock, 2008), 125–48.

CHAPTER 3

WORSHIP:
The Beginning and End of Mission

We have established that the missio Dei provides the essential theo-logical outlook for missional preaching, while a kingdom hermeneutic furnishes its essential biblical outlook. But one other essential remains: a liturgical perspective that affirms the unity of worship and mission. Sadly, worship activities and mission activities run on separate tracks in many churches, as if worship has little to do with mission, and vice versa. Many churches have committees devoted to worship and mission, demonstrating that they know the crucial nature of each. But little consultation happens between them. In a 1966 book titled *Worship & Mission,* J. G. Davies noted that the two "are placed in isolated compartments without the possibility of cross-fertilization and without the question of their unity being raised at all."[1] It should disturb us that something said as a prophetic charge nearly fifty years ago still largely applies today.

I took on a part-time worship pastor position at a church several years ago. To start off on the right foot, I flew to Dallas to attend a large worship conference. From morning to evening, the participants (over two thousand of us) feasted on music, keynote speakers, and an array of workshops par excellence. For the first few days, I thoroughly enjoyed myself. But around the third day, something began to gnaw at me, enough that I left the chandeliered ballroom before another service was about to begin and went up to the quiet of my hotel room to try to understand what was troubling my spirit. In the silence I heard the prophet Amos thunder the word of the Lord, "Take away from me the noise of your songs; I will not listen to the melody of your harps. But let justice roll down like waters, and righteousness like an ever-flowing stream" (Amos 5:23-24). Hearing these words, I reflected on the fact that I was only a few months removed from almost a decade of mission work among the desperately poor in the Philippines. Consequently, the absence of any references to compassion, justice, and good news for the poor while we sought "the heart of God" at this conference was like partaking of dessert in super-size portions for several days without eating anything else. No wonder my spiritual stomach was upset! The sweet bitterness of worship without mission made me nauseous. I stayed in my room and quietly whispered with tears the famous pledge of World Vision founder Bob Pierce, "Let my heart be broken by the things that break the heart of God."[2]

I attended another conference that same year, a gathering of about one hundred Asian mission theologians in Bangalore, India. My missionary self thrived there in the beginning, as I interacted with like-minded activists to address oppression, poverty, and religious pluralism in Asia. The problem was, except for occasional prayer, no serious effort was made by the organizers to ground mission in any kind of meaningful worship. As with the previous conference, I left feeling largely unfulfilled, as I remembered passages like, "On that day many will say to me, 'Lord, Lord, did we not prophesy . . . cast out demons . . . and do many deeds of power in your name?' Then I will declare to them, 'I never knew you . . .'" (Matt. 7:23).

Such practiced disunity between worship and mission reflects an ill-fated ignorance regarding the absolutely integral relationship between loving God (worship) and loving neighbor (mission). We who seek to be missional in our proclamation must address this ignorance, even as we strive to see more clearly the twin nature of worship and mission. What exactly is the relationship between them, and how should it inform the church's liturgy? More importantly for this study, why is this liturgical unity essential to missional preaching?

The Unity of Worship and Mission

The unity of worship and mission permeates the whole of Scripture, from the upward and outward nature of the Ten Commandments

(Ex. 20:1-17) to the prophets' dual call to spiritual fidelity and social justice (Hos. 3:1-5; Isa. 1:12-17) to the apostles' acts of ecstatic praise and fervent missionary zeal throughout the known world (Acts 2). But we encounter this unity most clearly in Jesus himself who, when asked by a testy lawyer which commandment was the greatest, replied: "'You shall love the Lord your God with all your heart, and with all your soul, and with all your mind.' This is the greatest and first commandment. And a second is like it: 'You shall love your neighbor as yourself.' On these two commandments hang all the law and the prophets" (Matt. 22:37-40).

Loving God lies at the core of the definition of *worship*. This truth is what allows New Testament scholar N. T. Wright to playfully substitute the word *love* with the word *worship* in the famous love chapter of 1 Corinthians 13. "Though we sing with the tongues of men and of angels, if we are not truly worshiping the living God, we are noisy gongs and clanging symbols," and so on, ending with, "So now our tasks are worship, mission, and management, these three; but the greatest of these is worship."[3]

Similarly, loving neighbor lies at the core of the definition of *mission*. If loving the lost and caring for the poor are driven by something less than love, then mission misses the mark entirely. "Love does not ask, 'Who is my neighbor?'" writes C. Rene Padilla, "but rather, 'Who needs me to be a good neighbor?' Who needs to hear the liberating news of the gospel? Who is in need of forgiveness? Who is suffering from the lack of food? Who is suffering the injustice of the system? Who needs our help? What can I do?"[4] Such questions are driven by the power of love extended to the lost and the poor in the world.

Speaking of love for God and love for neighbor separately, as I just did, already treads on dangerous ground. Since Jesus expanded the *Shema* by placing Deuteronomy 6:5 and Leviticus 19:18 together in one breath, love for God and neighbor are inextricably linked. "To love God then," concludes Melba Maggay, "is to love our neighbor, and to love our neighbor is to love God."[5] Each verifies and proves the other to be present in our lives and in our churches. That is, we know we truly love God when, out of love, we live out the gospel among the needy. And conversely, we know that when we love and serve the needy via works of compassion and mercy, we correspondingly love God in Jesus Christ (see Matt. 25:31-46).

Love God—Love Neighbor

The inseparability of loving God and neighbor correlates with the inseparability of worship and mission. There are at least two ways to describe the relationship between worship and mission.

Interdependent Unity

First, worship and mission enjoy an interdependent unity. Worship depends on mission, and mission depends on worship. If we try to love God (worship) while neglecting justice then God's words through the prophets Amos (5:21-23), Micah (6:6-8), and Isaiah (1:11-17) indict us. "We see in the language of the prophets," asserts Mark Labberton, "that faithful worship either does justice or [it] risks being neither faithful nor worship."[6] In the words of Amos, we are to "let justice roll down like waters and righteousness like an ever-flowing stream,"—and *then* come and worship!

If, on the other hand, we try to love our neighbor without being fueled and refueled by God in worship, then mission is rendered ineffectual. How can the church possibly address the overwhelming needs of the world without the input of God's wisdom, power, and love? Brenda Salter McNeil and Rick Richardson lament, "Far too often those who seek to be reconcilers and peacemakers have anemic worship—both individually and corporately." The authors go on to say that the "process of renewal and transformation takes place in worship and prepares us to be prophets who criticize the world's status quo, and it energizes the imagination for what is possible through God."[7] Simply put, if the church does not engage in mission, then it cannot truly worship; conversely, if the church does not worship, then it cannot truly do mission.

Causal Unity

Second, worship and mission have a causal unity between them; that is, one causes the other. The order in which Jesus lists the two Great Commandments is significant, because love for God (worship) is the source of love for neighbor (mission). Jesus' language in speaking of the "first" and "second" Great Commandments does not speak to superiority so much as origin—which of the two loves causes the other. To be clear: Worship inspires, motivates, and empowers mission. The church's love for God propels it outward to demonstrate love for neighbor.

Furthermore, worship is also the goal of mission. So worship not only gives birth to mission; it also represents the final fulfillment of mission at the end of time. John Piper's thoughts on their relationship are helpful here:

> Mission is not the ultimate goal of the church. Worship is. Mission exists because worship doesn't. . . . When this age is over, and the countless millions of the redeemed fall on their faces before the throne of God, mission will be no more. It is a temporary necessity. But worship abides forever. Worship, therefore, is the fuel and goal of mission.[8]

The worship scenes described in Revelation 7:9-12 and 19:1-8 will come about because of the faithfulness of the church in mission. The worship scenes in these two passages imply the sacrificial activities of God's people toward racial reconciliation, social justice, and evangelization, each of which plays a role in determining the ultimate worship-to-be at the end of time—a redeemed, multicultural people praising the God who has eradicated the evils of injustice, oppression, falsehood, greed, and immorality.[9] So worship causes mission; it simultaneously pushes it out and pulls it forward toward the end of time. Put succinctly, worship is both the beginning and the end of mission.

Missional Liturgy

This interdependent and causal unity of worship and mission should—must—inform the church's liturgy. Liturgy, conventionally understood, refers to the structure or order of worship when God's people gather together. Contrary to the notion that some churches are liturgical and others are not, all churches practice some form of liturgy (which is determined not only by tradition but also by culture).[10] As Colin Buchanan notes, "Even those who often have appeared most distrustful of the alleged straitjacketing of worship . . . have their own settled (but often undeclared) orders of Sunday worship with recognized patterns of use for songs and hymnody, and familiar acclamatory and responsive words."[11] That said, the worship in some churches is obviously more formally ordered than in others. Nevertheless, from the "bells and smells" of high church worship to the holy rolling of a Pentecostal-style service, all Christian liturgies include some form of a) prayer, b) music and song, c) word, and d) symbol (sacraments or ordinances), all of which are experienced in the context of *koinonia*.[12]

In light of the unity of worship and mission, "the liturgy of corporate worship will impact . . . the corporate mission of the people *as they gather in order to be sent out*."[13] Liturgy, therefore, is ultimately the practice of missional worship. At its root, the word *liturgy* means "the work of the people," and this work does not end when the Sunday service is over. The work of the people—the liturgy—must be practiced, yes, in corporate gatherings, but also in our everyday lives as we engage the world in mission. Mission, according to the Eastern Orthodox statement "Go Forth in Peace," is the "liturgy after the liturgy."[14]

So how does this outlook inform the church's practice of worship? Prayers of the people would not be limited to the needs of the Body, but extended to include the community and world. Songs would inspire people to adore God for who God is, to give thanks for all God has done and will do, and to pledge allegiance to God's kingdom for the sake of the whole world. The ministry of the Word would recite Scriptures (which we established earlier as thoroughly missional) and preaching would lift up their missional dimensions (more on this aspect, of course, in a little while). And the experience of ritual symbols—i.e., the tactile and visual expressions of worship such as baptism and Communion—would invoke remembrance of Christ's loving sacrifice for the whole world and would, therefore, inspire loving sacrifice among worshipers as they follow him to the cross for the sake of the world.

I do not suggest these things formulaically and mechanically, as if we are required to force "mission" on each and every part of the service. In fact, I champion more creative license in the church's liturgy-making. However, a Creator-glorifying, Christ-centered, Spirit-empowered worship service necessarily progresses toward a call to participate in God's mission. For example, evangelism scholar Paul Chilcote offers a "sequence of devotion" based upon the well-known vision of Isaiah 6:1-8:

1. Adoration: "Holy, holy, holy is the Lord of hosts," moves the worshiper to
2. Confession: "Woe is me!" to
3. Forgiveness: "Your guilt has departed and your sin is blotted out," and through

4. Proclamation: "Then I heard the voice of the Lord saying,"
   to final
5. Dedication: "Here am I; send me!"[15]

The point is, whether every aspect of the liturgy speaks directly of mission or the whole service crescendos at mission, God's redemptive purposes and our participation in them are constitutive of authentic Christian worship.

In light of the missional vision of the practice of worship, it should be obvious that missional liturgy is not necessarily a call to design services in order to reach unbelievers. (I think critically of the seeker-friendly phenomenon of the 1980s and 90s, as well as some churches' need to have an altar call in every service.) "Worship must remain worship," cautions Roberta King. "Worship services should not serve as functional substitutes for evangelism. Rather, we must seek authenticity of interaction with God and developing relationship with him."[16] But she goes on to say that, "Genuine worship of the Creator will attract and confront those who long to enter into the kingdom."[17]

The vision for missional liturgy is rather a call for all churches to practice worship's oneness with God's mission. The experience of corporate Christian worship should, in its totality, not only give glory to God; it should also clarify the *missio Dei* and our participation in it, even as the redeemed themselves are transformed by the worship experience. "Somehow," Labberton pleads, "the God we name, the music we sing, the prayers we offer, and the Scriptures we hear read and preached [have] to call us deeper into God's heart and deeper into the world for which Christ died."[18]

Missional Preaching in the Practice of Worship

The importance of adopting such a liturgy for missional preaching lies in the truth that the *kerygma* by itself cannot reshape the church for mission. The Word part of the liturgy is exactly that—only a part of the whole experience of corporate worship. As Marva Dawn states, "A sermon finds its place in the midst of the community's entire worship."[19] Therefore, the effectiveness of the missional sermon relies on a missionally framed service, each aspect working together to glorify God and to better understand God's purposes in and for the world.

Although preaching is but one part, it is a key part in the worship experience of God's people. In Roman Catholic, Anglican, Lutheran, and Eastern Orthodox traditions, the Eucharist (Communion or the Lord's Supper) is central to community worship; but in most Protestant traditions, it is the ministry of the Word that occupies the center. In fact, for many Protestants, if a sermon or homily or meditation is not part of the gathering, it is "worship lite" at best—perhaps not even worship at all! Few Christians would argue that preaching plays an indispensable role in the church's practice of worship.

Specifically, the role of preaching in missional liturgy entails the clear articulation of God and God's mission. An excellently preached word articulates—makes clear—God's intentions like no song, ritual, or prayer could. Missional preaching has the capacity to explain, define, exhort, inspire, and connect all other aspects of the service toward a greater understanding of the *missio Dei*.

As the unity of worship and mission informs the church's liturgy, some guiding principles for preaching emerge.

Personal Preparation

First, we prepare ourselves to lead worship missionally. This requires more than intellectual agreement with the theological unity of worship and mission. It requires our commitment to grow in this unity on our own with God. Labberton shares his regular practice of reading the weekly email update from a missionary family serving at-risk children in Cambodia before Sunday service, because he writes, "I want . . . to lead our worship services . . . with my heart freshly reminded of the realities of suffering in the world, the urgency of hearing and living out the hope of the gospel, and the joyous and costly call of sacrificial living in the name of Christ."[20] As we grow in this unity, we prepare ourselves to lead God's people accordingly.

Being Thoroughly Missional

Second, we see to it that the whole service reflects the awareness that the God who longs to redeem creation and everyone in it is present. Preaching alone will not suffice. But if every aspect of the service points in the same direction, when it is time to preach a word imbibed with mission, the people will be poised to receive it, since everything else has been speaking the same language. Insofar as the order of service lies in the hands of the ministers—and in most churches, that is the case—those who seek to give a compelling missional word should seek to ensure that the rest of the service will support it.

Cultivating Disciples

Finally, we preach with the aim to make disciples. We preach to cultivate a church of missional worshipers and worshiping missionaries, people who understand that their experience of worship directly affects their practice of the faith in the world, and vice versa. We preach to build a church that understands that the work of compassion, justice, reconciliation, and evangelization requires a power that is derived only from a life connected to the living God.

To cultivate such disciples, however, entails, in Dawn's words, preaching that kills us. She writes, "Everything that we do in worship should kill us, but especially the part of the service in which we hear the Word—the Scripture lessons and the sermon."[21] She means here that true worship, expressed most clearly in the ministry of the Word, results in the death of self and the resurrection to new life in Christ, a life that calls us to community and mission. Similarly, the truth that genuine worship leads to sacrificial mission for the sake of the lost and the poor in the world explains why Labberton can describe worship as a "dangerous act." He writes, "Nothing is as dangerous as encountering the living God. Why? Because meeting God redefines everything we call normal and commands us to seek first his kingdom."[22] This kind of preaching in the context of a missional liturgy will indeed produce missional worshipers and worshiping missionaries—that is, genuine disciples. At that point, the positively dangerous power of the gospel through a faithful church is released into the world.

NOTES

1. J. G. Davies, *Worship & Mission* (London, UK: SCM, 1966), 9.
2. Bob Pierce, quoted in Marilee Pierce Dunker, *Man of Vision* (Waynesboro, GA: Authentic; Federal Way, WA: World Vision, 2005), 1.
3. N. T. Wright, *For All God's Worth: True Worship and the Calling of the Church* (Grand Rapids: Eerdmans, 1997), 8–9.
4. C. Rene Padilla, "Love," in *Dictionary of Mission Theology*, ed. John Corrie (Downers Grove: IVP Academic, 2007), 213.
5. Melba Maggay, "To Respond to Human Need by Loving Service (i)," in *Mission in the 21st Century*, eds. Andrew Walls and Cathy Ross (Maryknoll, NY: Orbis, 2008), 47.
6. Mark Labberton, *The Dangerous Act of Worship: Living God's Call to Justice* (Downers Grove: IVP, 2007), 28.

7. Brenda Salter McNeil and Rick Richardson, *The Heart of Racial Justice: How Soul Change Leads to Social Change* (Downers Grove: IVP, 2004), 61.

8. John Piper, *Let the Nations Be Glad: The Supremacy of God in Missions* (Grand Rapids: Baker, 1993), 11. I took the liberty here to replace "missions" with "mission." There has been bantering back and forth about the difference between these two words among missiologists through the years, but most people use them interchangeably.

9. For more on this idea, see Al Tizon, "A Spirituality of Holistic Ministry," *inMinistry* (Spring 2010), 15.

10. See Kathy Black, *Worship across Cultures: A Handbook* (Nashville: Abingdon, 1998).

11. Colin O. Buchanan, "Liturgy," in *Dictionary of Mission Theology*, ed. John Corrie (Downers Grove: IVP Academic, 2007), 211.

12. Stanley J. Grenz, *Theology for the Community of God* (Grand Rapids: Eerdmans; Vancouver, BC: Regent College, 1994), 492–95.

13. Buchanan, "Liturgy," 212. Emphasis mine.

14. "Go Forth in Peace," in *New Directions in Mission & Evangelization 1: Basic Statements 1974–1991*, eds. James A. Scherer and Stephen B. Bevans (Maryknoll, NY: Orbis, 1992), 226ff.

15. Paul W. Chilcote, "The Integral Nature of Worship and Evangelism," in *The Study of Evangelism: Exploring a Missional Practice of the Church*, eds. Paul W. Chilcote and Laceye C. Warner (Grand Rapids: Eerdmans, 2008), 253–61.

16. Roberta R. King, "Worship," in *Evangelical Dictionary of World Missions*, ed. A. Scott Moreau (Grand Rapids: Baker; Carlisle, Cumbria, UK: Paternoster, 2000), 1035.

17. King, "Worship," 1035.

18. Labberton, *The Dangerous Act of Worship*, 35.

19. Marva Dawn, *Reaching Out without Dumbing Down: A Theology of Worship for the Turn-of-the-Century Church* (Grand Rapids: Eerdmans, 1995), 233.

20. Labberton, *The Dangerous Act of Worship*, 33–34.

21. Dawn, *Reaching Out without Dumbing Down*, 206.

22. Labberton, *The Dangerous Act of Worship*, 63.

PART 2

The Goals
of Missional Preaching

"If you aim at nothing, you will hit it every time," says the well-known adage. Now that we have considered the essentials that make missional preaching possible—a theological outlook that affirms the missional nature of God's very being (*missio Dei*), an approach to the Bible that sees God's redemptive purposes throughout its pages (missional hermeneutic), and a practical grasp of the unity of worship and mission (missional liturgy)—we need to consider the goals of this type of preaching. We need to aim carefully to ensure that we hit the target.

I find it interesting and a little disturbing that the language of goals is rarely invoked in homiletical discussions. What do we hope to accomplish in our preaching? I am not referring here to individual sermons (although I've heard not a few sermons that could have used a point). Rather, I am referring to fundamental goals that, when striven for, help determine the theological, ethical, and practical—in a word, *missional*—shape of the church.

When we lack clarity about where we want to lead God's people in our preaching and teaching, our churches all too often take on the shape of the surrounding culture. So in that sense, the adage breaks down; if we aim at nothing in our preaching, we end up being right on target for taking on the shape of prevailing culture. Now culture, as we shall see in Chapter 4, is not something to repudiate, but to love and serve. Yet this happens not when we blindly conform to the surrounding culture but when we transform it through the prophetic power of the gospel. Developing goals for our preaching will empower the church to communicate with culture without coming to look and act just like all that surrounds us.

If the first section of this book has been convincing at all, then we would agree that the goals of our preaching must be missional in nature. What are the desired outcomes of missional preaching? As I reflect upon my life as a missionary, activist, pastor, and professor, at least seven goals emerge that have defined my hopes as I serve the church in preaching and teaching:

- **Inculturation** (a theological adaptation of *enculturation*) amid an us-and-them mentality
- **Alternative community** amid cultural conformity
- **Holistic transformation** amid a false dichotomy of evangelism and social concern
- **Justice and reconciliation** amid gender, race, and class privilege
- **Whole-life stewardship** amid materialism, consumerism, and environmental abuse
- **Consistent life and peace** *(Shalom)* amid violence and death
- **Uniqueness and universality of Christ** (**Scandal of Jesus**) amid religious pluralism.

This list probably does not exhaust the goals of missional preaching; on the other hand, in considering the mission-oriented sermons I have delivered or heard in my life, I am hard pressed to think of one that is not directed toward one of these goals. If our preaching can help shape our congregations to conform to the image suggested by these goals, I believe we will be helping the church conform to the image of God and God's mission.

These goals are large and certainly cannot be achieved in a single sermon or even a single series (although—*hint, hint*—they would make for a good, initial series to give a bird's-eye view that sets the tone for mission). Rather these goals define the missional character of the church and, therefore, the direction in which missional preachers need to aim.

CHAPTER 4

PREACHING FOR
Inculturation

Shortly after my wife, Janice, and I arrived in the Philippines, our mission agency placed us in the home of a Filipino family in a poor barrio on the outskirts of Manila.[1] We resisted the idea at first, appealing to the fact that we had two young children—a five-year-old daughter and a one-year-old son. Such living arrangements would be too difficult for them, we argued. Truth be told, we wondered if it would be too difficult for the two of *us*! The language barrier, the completely alien culture, and the hardships of barrio life would make for an unnecessarily difficult time. Our middle-class fears mounted a moderate resistance to the idea of bonding, a process that missiologists Tom and Betty Sue Brewster have applied to newly arriving missionaries, borrowing the idea from the necessary bonding between newborn and parent within the animal kingdom. New missionaries are like infants born into a whole new world, who are "in a state of unique readiness, both physiologically and emotionally, to become a belonger with the local people."[2] The mission agency, which at that time required all its new missionaries "to bond," smoothly overcame our objections and sent us off to live with what turned out to be a warm and hospitable family in a small barrio called Biga in the province of Cavite. We had a wonderful time.

Don't get me wrong: It was not easy. The giant spiders we heard shuffling on the ground near our bamboo beds at night, the treacherous hill to get to the river where the people washed their clothes, the foods our systems were not used to, the mosquitoes that bit us (yes, we used repellent), the oppressive heat, and the fact that we were not able to communicate with anyone—all these made for one of the hardest weeks of our lives. The sanitized, middle-class, suburban life this was not! Yet we wouldn't trade that experience for anything. In fact, it galvanized our commitment to do mission, not from afar, not from the infamous colonial mission compound, not from Western condescension, but from a place of learning and serving with, for, and among the people. The Brewsters were right; we "bonded" with the Filipino people, which led us to strive to engage in mission contextually and authentically. We certainly committed our share of cultural *faux pas*, but we did our best to learn from our mistakes as we participated as fully as we could in the local culture.

From my own experience of the bonding process, I can vouch for its effectiveness in helping missionaries commit to full contextual engagement, or what has been called *inculturation*. And lest anyone think inculturation applies only to missionaries going off to exotic lands, let me clearly state that it applies to Christians everywhere. The "mission compound," where foreign missionaries "eat their own food, wear their own style of clothes, talk their own language, educate their children with their own curriculum, etc. [behind] . . . high walls and locked gates . . . away from the people of the host culture," is not limited to the traditional mission field.[3] The proclivity of U.S. Christians to create their own subculture within the larger culture—i.e., interacting primarily with one another, making friends primarily among themselves, patronizing only Christian businesses, listening only to Christian music, and developing their own "Christian-ese"—is its own North American version of the "mission compound."

Missional preaching challenges this disposition. It rejects the us-and-them frame of mind that the compound mentality creates. More positively, it aims to call the people of God to engage the culture fully, to embrace it, to become insiders so we might communicate the gospel not just by the words we say but by the loving, accepting lives we live. It aims to equip the church to inculturate.

Inculturation and Incarnation

Inculturation is a funny word; standard dictionaries certainly would not include it. In the 1970s, Catholic missiologists coined the term, which combines the anthropological process of enculturation with the theological truth of Christ's incarnation.[4] This synthetic word conveys the establishment of real presence in a community by virtue of the mutual embrace of missionary and host culture.[5]

For the missionary, it involves learning the heart language (verbal and nonverbal), life-ways, values, beliefs, and history of the culture. Furthermore and most important, the missionary embraces the culture with a commitment to establish real relationships with the people. Inculturation conveys a process by which gospel-bearers fully identify with the people they feel called to serve. "To the Jews, I became as a Jew, in order to win Jews," wrote the apostle Paul. "I have become all things to all people, so that I might by any means save some" (1 Cor. 9:20-22). Inculturation is the process of knowing culture intimately and deeply. It is responsible, sensitive, humble, committed border-crossing. It is full-life immersion. It is going native.

The word *incarnation* and its various forms ("incarnational," "incarnational ministry," and even "reincarnation") have become a part of the *lingua franca* of the missional movement.[6] In the 1970s, missiologists began using this term as another synonym for *inculturation* and *contextualization*,[7] and it has become the overwhelming word of choice for the contemporary missional movement. It is often employed by urban ministry practitioners who intentionally relocate in impoverished neighborhoods in order to flesh out the gospel among the poor.[8]

These urban missionaries take their cue from mentors such as John and Vera Mae Perkins, who left a life of comfort and success in California to return to Mississippi in order to be good news to the poor and marginalized among fellow African Americans in the South.[9] Other mentors include Viv Grigg, a New Zealander who lived and served in a squatter community in Metro-Manila in the 1980s, catalyzing a global movement of "incarnational missionaries."[10] The list would also include Wayne and Anne Gordon, who moved into the notoriously dangerous neighborhood of North Lawndale in Chicago, which has resulted in one of the finest examples of local church-based community transformation in the country.[11]

But at a more fundamental level, these urban missionaries who have chosen to relocate are following the example of Jesus Christ, the Son of God, who chose to become a human being in order to reach humanity (John 1:1-3, 14). God could have safely communicated the gospel from above, throwing tracts down from heaven or broadcasting the message by divine satellite or just continuing to send new prophets to replace the ones the world would kill. God chose instead to understand and relate to us by becoming one of us. This amazing truth, among other things, has served as an example for God's people to incarnate (or, if you will, reincarnate) into the cultures to which God has called them. Church consultant Alan Hirsch, who has coined the term *missional-incarnational,* explains: "If God's central way of reaching the world was to incarnate himself in Jesus, then our way of reaching the world should likewise be incarnational."[12]

I personally prefer the term *inculturation* over *incarnation,* despite my use of the latter as much as anyone in much of my speaking and writing. When I think long and hard about it, I become reticent to use the same term that describes the Word-made-flesh in Jesus Christ to also describe the process of crossing cultures. *Inculturation* is a little more modest, as it acknowledges the human element in the process. It is more humble and honest; to be missional is not to incarnate but to inculturate. But I will stop quibbling over words now (an occupational hazard!), except to say that if one word encourages humility over the other, I would encourage us to choose that one. At the end of the day, both terms (and all the other ones) attempt to get at the same practice—namely, to bear witness to the gospel, not as alien outsiders, but as learned insiders.

Preaching that calls God's people to inculturate summons us to understand, be a part of, suffer, rejoice, and fall in love with the culture we seek to transform. Conversely, it means avoiding a condescending, judgmental, us-and-them posture. Preaching for inculturation takes seriously issues that are important and relevant to the culture, and calls the community of disciples to participate in that culture with humility, respect, and love.

Characteristics of an Inculturated Life

Insofar as goals are supposed to be measurable, how can we discern if the message of inculturation is getting through? We who are inspired by the gospel to fully engage our culture embody at least six characteristics.

Real Relationships with Real People

First and foremost, inculturation demands forming real relationships with people outside the church. The key word here is *real,* as this characteristic flies in the face of developing relationships based upon evangelistic manipulation, i.e., "I'm going to befriend you in order to convert you." Inculturation calls God's people to go beyond the walls of the church and form genuine relationships with atheistic colleagues, lapsed Christians, alcoholic neighbors, and promiscuous classmates, and to do so not as problem-free, struggle-free, doubt-free followers of Jesus, but as "one beggar telling another beggar where to find food."[13] As inculturated people, we do not separate ourselves from the world of the unchurched; rather, we go to the movies, share meals, encourage one another's children to play together, discuss politics and sports, listen, share, cry, and laugh with those who are considered the Other. We befriend and allow ourselves to be befriended in a genuine way.

Cultural and Political Participation

Second, inculturated lives participate in the political and cultural life of the community. This is where knowledge of local issues, participating in local (and national) elections, and being involved in cultural events enter into the picture. The inculturated are engaged on these levels. The un-inculturated know only what's going on in the church community and are largely unconcerned about, perhaps even antagonistic toward, what's going on in the rest of the community.

For example, we encountered many churches in the Philippines that prohibited their members from participating in their local fiesta celebrations each year, citing that these gatherings venerate the patron saint of the given town. Leaders also prohibited members from going to the cemetery on All Saints Day, saying Christians should not be identified with those who commune with the dead. The rest of the community viewed the churches' sitting-out as judgmental and condemning. They became known in many communities as the "Born-Against Christians." While there should certainly be awareness of what lies behind such events, we as inculturated people participate in political issues and cultural events while remaining faithful to who we are in Christ.

Knowledge of Community History

Third, we have some grasp of the history of our communities. For instance, I have found it helpful to know that the township of Upper Darby, Pennsylvania, where my family and I currently live, was a predominantly Irish- and Italian-American community until about twenty-five years ago. Since the mid-1980s, Asian-, African-, and Latino-Americans have gradually moved into the neighborhoods. Immigrants from Greece and more recently from Liberia and other African countries have also poured in, to the point where Upper Darby is now a showcase of the increasingly diversifying, first-ring suburbs of the United States.[14]

Such historical perspective has helped me understand, for example, why the leadership of the town's institutions, from the municipal council to the school board, remains almost all white. The township as a whole still seems a little shell-shocked at the remarkable rate of demographic change taking place within its borders. (At least, that is part of the reason.) In time and with intentional transition management, I am confident that the town's institutions will eventually reflect the richness of its diversifying population; at least that is my hope. Inculturated persons take the time to understand a community's past in order to know its present situation better, thereby learning to be sensitive, responsible agents of change.

Vulnerability

Fourth, as inculturated persons, we open ourselves up to be helped, served, and changed by the culture. This is perhaps the most dangerous of the characteristics, for it acknowledges the risk that comes with inculturation. As we embrace the surrounding culture, we will come face to face with all the good and the bad of that culture. The risk we take to bear witness incarnationally to the transforming gospel is that we leave ourselves vulnerable to being transformed by the culture. If we are truly in relationship with people, then insofar as the gospel is contagious to them, whatever beliefs, ideas, and practices they embody are contagious to us.

Inculturation gone awry results in either *cultural accommodation*—when a church looks, acts, and believes just like culture and thereby becomes irrelevant—or *syncretism*—when the church becomes a fascinating but distorted expression of the faith, as unchanged cultural beliefs and practices are wrapped in symbols and images that are barely recognizable to biblical faith.[15] Dare we take such a risk? Inculturation says, "Yes, absolutely!" Of course, we must take precautions, but such a risk is inherent in genuine, relational gospel-bearing.[16]

Identification with the Poor and Marginalized

Fifth, inculturated lives form authentic relationships with those most vulnerable in the community. The Incarnation did not just reveal God's desire to communicate with humanity; it also revealed God's desire to associate especially with the lowly, the poor, and the marginalized of humanity. From a barnyard birth (Matt. 1:18ff; Luke 2:1ff) to rural village existence as the son of a laborer (Luke 2:39), from eating with tax collectors, prostitutes, and sinners (Matt. 9:10ff) to conversing with outcasts (John 4:1ff) to healing the sick and demon-possessed (Matt. 9:35), Jesus demonstrated that the living truth of the Incarnation carries with it identification with the vulnerable in society, the underdogs. I will say more about this in Chapter 7; for now, let it suffice to say that as inculturated persons we develop a keen awareness of the "invisible" in society and proactively seek them out.

Love for Culture

Finally, inculturated people have learned to love the culture. Renowned Christian urbanologist Ray Bakke states, "We cannot work in our city unless we love it—its architecture, sewer system, politics, history, traditions and neighborhoods."[17] This love for place and its people applies not just to the city, but to any and every place God calls us. This love is ultimately what makes the church a cultural insider, which is important because only insiders have the right to critique and participate in the transformation of culture.

While serving in the Philippines, I developed an acute intolerance for new missionaries who, shortly after arriving, began to complain, judge, and look down upon Filipinos and their culture. *It's so dirty and smoggy. The people don't know how to run things. The educational system is horrible. Government is so corrupt.* And so on. I increasingly resented such sentiments, partly because I was rediscovering my own ethnicity as a Filipino and found the complaints of foreigners to be personally insulting, but also because, in my mind, their complaining automatically disqualified them from doing what they came to do—namely, to bear witness to the gospel in loving service of the Filipino. We cannot serve and reach people whom we do not love. Love of place and its people is, in fact, the ultimate characteristic of genuine inculturation.

Preaching for Inculturation

As we hone these six characteristics of inculturation into principles for preaching, three basic guidelines come to the surface.

Real Presence

Foundationally, we preach to establish the church's presence in the community. The church needs to be present, swimming in the mainstream with the rest of the culture and developing positive relationships with people in the workplace, the marketplace, and the streets. The church needs to be a good neighbor. This is not so much a call to be liked but a call to be in genuine relationship with people as a demonstration of God's relational love for the world. Conversely, we preach against relational otherworldliness—that is, against sincere but inappropriate behavior, which is supposedly done in the name of Jesus but which repels instead of attracts. I think of acts ranging from aggressive "street witnessing" to using churchy language such as "Praise the Lord" and "Jesus saves" at the office. Preaching for inculturation equips God's people to be real, to be in relationship, to be invited to water-cooler conversations, all the while remaining faithful to who we are in Christ.

Participation in the Public Square

We also preach the gospel's implications to the issues relevant to the culture, equipping God's people to participate in public issues humbly, respectfully, and lovingly. Preaching for inculturation not only calls the church to be good neighbors; it also calls it to responsible citizenry. It does not hide behind the misconception that the church is supposed to be apolitical. Most churches understand that word to mean to stay out of the fray, when it really means the church should never be too closely aligned with any one political party or candidate.

During the 2008 presidential elections, our church hosted a gathering of church and community members to discuss the convictions and promises of the candidates. Using ESA's booklet *Politics and the Bible,*[18] I guided the discussion, doing my best to stick to the issues and to discourage comments on the candidates' personal lives (as if we really knew anything about their personal lives in the first place!). It was three hours of good food, strong opinions, and civil disagreement. Both Democrats and Republicans, along with a few

Independents, were present. And as a result, various positions were represented and expressed. It was a night that our congregation, which served as host to the event, hoped would demonstrate socio-political engagement without declaring a singular "biblical position" on any issue or endorsing "God's choice" among the candidates. For the most part, I believe we succeeded. Preaching for inculturation challenges the "apolitical position" as it is often used; the church *needs* to be in the fray. In fact, it needs to help shape the fray!

Sacrifice and Lifestyle

Ultimately, we preach to call the people of God to lose themselves for the sake of others, especially the poor and downtrodden. If the cross, which Jesus bore for the sake of all, teaches us anything, it is sacrificial love. In the words of the Master, "If any want to become my followers, let them deny themselves and take up their cross and follow me" (Mark 8:34). To inculturate means fleshing out the gospel in our lives. This means *not* fleshing out the pursuit of wealth, comfort, prestige, etc. For some it means relocating to hard, dangerous places in order to establish relational presence. For others it means becoming a foster parent or volunteering regularly at a homeless shelter or nursing home. For all, it means committing to a simpler lifestyle as a personal act of solidarity with the less fortunate in the world (more on this in Chapter 8). Preaching for inculturation finally calls each of us to cross-bearing sacrifice as we identify with the lost and the least for the sake of the good news of God's reign.

■ ■ ■

In "Re-formed Heart, Open Homes," missionary Ruth Padilla De-Borst provides an example of a sermon that calls for inculturation, as she expounds upon the powerful story of Peter and Cornelius in Acts 10. How does it challenge us to affirm and engage culture, particularly cultures that have been marginalized and stigmatized? And how does it instruct us to cross cultures for the sake of the gospel?

NOTES

1. Janice and I served as missionaries to the Philippines (where I am originally from) under the auspices of an interdenominational mission agency called Action International Ministries from 1989 to 1998.

2. E. Thomas Brewster and Elizabeth S. Brewster, *Bonding and the Missionary Task: Establishing a Sense of Belonging* (Pasadena, CA: Lingua House, 1984), 4.

3. Ronald J. Sider, John M. Perkins, Wayne L. Gordon, F. Albert Tizon, *Linking Arms, Linking Lives: How Urban-Suburban Partnerships Can Transform Communities* (Grand Rapids, MI: Baker, 2008), 102–103.

4. For a more detailed treatment of the term, see Arji Roest Crollius, "Inculturation," in *Following Christ in Mission*, ed., Sebastian Karotemprel (Pasay City, Philippines: Paulines, 1996), 110–119. A synonym for *inculturation* is *contextualization*, a term generally preferred by Protestant missiologists. See Darrell Whiteman, "Contextualization: The Theory, the Gap, the Challenge, *International Bulletin of Missionary Research* 21/1 (January 1997), 2–7. Older terms like *adaptation, accommodation,* and *indigenization* have essentially run their course.

5. Leonardo N. Mercado, *Inculturation and Filipino Theology* (Manila, Philippines: Divine Word, 1992), 18–39. I appreciate Mercado's definition of *inculturation* as a two-way process that involves not just the missionary, but also the host culture.

6. See for example, Michael Frost and Alan Hirsch, *The Shaping of Things to Come: Innovation and Mission for the 21st Century Church* (Peabody, MA: Hendrickson, 2003), 33–59.

7. James A. Scherer and Stephen B. Bevans, "Introduction," in *New Directions in Mission & Evangelization 3: Faith and Culture,* eds. James A. Scherer and Stephen B. Bevans (Maryknoll, NY: Orbis, 1999), 5.

8. See Bob Lupton, Peggy Lupton, and Gloria Yancey, "Relocation: Living in the Community," in *Restoring At-Risk Communities: Doing It Together and Doing It Right,* ed. John M. Perkins (Grand Rapids: Baker, 1996), 75–105. See also Scott A. Bessenecker, *The New Friars* (Downers Grove: IVP, 2008) and John B. Hayes, *Submerge: Living Deep in a Shallow World—Service, Justice and Contemplation Among the World's Poor* (Ventura, CA: Regal, 2006).

9. John M. Perkins, *Let Justice Roll Down* (Ventura, CA: Regal, 2006).

10. Viv Grigg, *Companion to the Poor* (Monrovia, CA: MARC, 1990). For more information about a mission organization inspired by Grigg called Servants to Asia's Poor, go to http://www.servantsasia.org/. See also Michael Duncan, *Costly Mission* (Monrovia: MARC, 1996); Jenny M. Craig, *Servants Among the Poor* (Mandaluyong City, Philippines: OMF Literature; Wellington, New Zealand: SERVANTS, 1998); Craig Greenfield, *The Urban Halo* (London, UK et al.: Authentic Media, 2007).

11. Wayne L. Gordon, *Real Hope in Chicago* (Grand Rapids: Zondervan, 1995). See also an outsider's perspective of Lawndale Community Church, of which Gordon serves as founding pastor, in Jim Henderson and Matt Casper, *Jim and Casper Go to Church* (Carol Stream, IL: Barna, 2007), 61–72.

12. Alan Hirsch, *The Forgotten Ways: Reactivating the Missional Church* (Grand Rapids: Brazos; New South Wales, Australia: Strand, 2006), 133.

13. This quote is attributed to the famous Indian evangelist D.T. Niles.

14. Sider et al., *Linking Arms, Linking Lives,* 31–32.

15. Tim Morey, *Embodying Our Faith: Becoming a Living, Sharing, Practicing Church* (Downers Grove: IVP, 2009), 77–80.

16. Paul G. Hiebert, *Anthropological Insights for Missionaries* (Grand Rapids: Baker Academic, 1986), 110. In this volume, Hiebert, an anthropologist, develops a framework for what he calls "critical contextualization." For a concise treatment of Hiebert's "critical contextualization," see Frost and Hirsch, *The Shaping of Things to Come,* 89–94.

17. Ray Bakke, *The Urban Christian: Effective Ministry in Today's Urban World* (Downers Grove: IVP, 1987), 63.

18. Ronald J. Sider, *Politics and the Bible: A Study Guide for Christians* (Wynnewood, PA: Evangelicals for Social Action, n.d.).

Re-formed Heart: Open Homes

■ ■ ■

Ruth Padilla DeBorst
ACTS 10:19-48

"Surely not, Lord! I have never eaten anything impure or unclean! What on earth is this?" Peter asks himself. "I should have gone down from the roof earlier. It is hot and my stomach is playing tricks on my mind! I got too hungry, and here I am, hallucinating. This cannot be from God."

But the voice is insisting: "Do not call anything impure that God has made clean."

"I do not understand. The law prohibits us as God's people from even touching such foul meat. Other people eat it, but not us! We know better!"

However, the large sheet, which contains all kinds of four-footed animals as well as reptiles of the earth and birds of the air, does not disappear, and the voice comes, repeatedly, incessant, insistent: "Get up, Peter. Kill and eat."

Baffling. Perturbing. But as Acts 10 and 11 record, Peter's experience was by no means simply the stray vision of a hungry man. The story describes an issue that threatened to wrench the early church apart. It illustrates the enormous paradigm shift the early church had to undergo in faithfulness to the God who is sovereign over all nations. It tells about what I see as the first real Reformation of the church.

A little context before learning more about this first Reformation: At the time Peter received this surprising message, he'd been feeling relieved. Yes, Christians were still being persecuted, but the church community was growing and becoming established. Some of the pesky internal matters of the beginning had been ironed out. The fate of the impostors, Ananias and Sapphira, had taught the community a serious ethical lesson. In addition, the church now had deacons who made sure everyone in the community was being well cared for—including the widows of the proselytes (those Gentiles who had chosen the Jewish religion and then had begun following Jesus). Peter's itinerant ministry among Jewish followers of Jesus was fruitful, and many among his people were turning to the Lord.

However, now, just when matters appeared to be somewhat under control, this perturbing sheet is hung down before him and the very purity of his Jewish identity is challenged. God began to reform Peter's heart:

> The next day [Peter] got up and went with [the men whom Cornelius sent] . . . . Cornelius was expecting them and had called together his relatives and close friends. On Peter's arrival Cornelius met him, and falling at his feet, worshipped him. But Peter made him get up, saying, "Stand up; I am only a mortal." And as he talked with him, he went in and found that many had assembled; and he said to them, "You yourselves know that it is unlawful for a Jew to associate with or to visit a Gentile; but God has shown me that I should not call anyone profane or unclean. So when I was sent for, I came without objection. . . ."
>
> Then Peter began to speak to them: "I truly understand that God shows no partiality, but in every nation anyone who fears him and does what is right is acceptable to him. . . ." While Peter was still speaking, the Holy Spirit fell upon all who heard the word. . . . So he ordered them to be baptized in the name of Jesus Christ. (Acts 10:23-48)

Cornelius had called to God and sought out Peter. He and his family heard the gospel as Peter preached; they received God's Spirit and were baptized. God was effecting a conversion in the heart of this Roman centurion and his household. And the heavens rejoiced that day!

But I dare say that the greater conversion was the one happening in Peter's heart. No longer could he conceive of himself and his fellow Jews as the only brokers of God's action in the world. Through his perplexing vision and his encounter with Cornelius, Peter caught a glimpse of God's heart for all people, regardless of nationality, gender, color, social standing, or economic status. His borders were being blasted open, and he became an emissary to the broader community of God's all-encompassing love for all people. No longer could he hold a leash on God's Spirit, restricting the gift only to people akin to him in religious tradition and ethnic background. He later explained to the other apostles, "God gave them"—i.e., the Gentiles, those the Jews had excluded—"the same gift as he gave us" (Acts 11:17). The same? Can anyone have the same value, giftedness, even closeness to God as us, God's chosen people? But we are IN, as in *insiders* and the others are OUT, as in *outsiders!*

Peter's vision set in motion the key struggle of the early church, as it attempted to come to grips with the radical implications of the equalizing and all-inclusive gospel. The good news of Christ was not only for Jews, but for all. Accepting this truth took time and struggle, as stories of controversy, condemnation, conflict, and church councils blend in with the stories of celebration, recognition, acceptance, and hospitality throughout the rest of the book of Acts and the whole of the New Testament.

It is well worth noting that the designation *Christian* was first attributed to the followers of Jesus not in Jerusalem, where the initial community had been established, but out on the margins, among these new believers in the multicultural and often looked-down-upon Gentile city of Antioch. In addition, and in spite of the prejudice often held against them by their fellow believers in Jerusalem, the Christians of Antioch ended up reaching out through a generous offering when the Jerusalem church was hit with famine and persecution (Acts 11:27-30).

Can you see why I refer to the story of Peter's encounter with Cornelius and the engagement of Jesus' first followers with the outsiders of their day as the first real Reformation? If this had not happened, then the Christian faith would have been just another Jewish sect; no Gentiles, except for perhaps a few who were willing to become Jews first, would have made up what developed in the centuries that followed as the Christian faith. If this story went another way, in all likelihood, we—Gentiles—might not be included in the Christian family.

But besides just being grateful that we have become partakers of the blessings of the gospel, what else does this story teach us? *Unclean* for Peter was Cornelius, that commander of the occupying army. And *unequal* for the first church were those outsiders who would not conform to their Jewish traditions. Who in the here-and-now, we must ask, are the "untouchables" that we as Christ's followers are called to embrace today?

There are many, but let me point out one group—undocumented immigrants. "Illegals," they are often called, simply because they hold no official documents. "Unclean" and "unequal" and "outsiders"— men, women, and children by the millions—fill the cities of this country. Most of them seek only worthy employment and a place to belong. The vast majority work long hours to support themselves and entire families back home. Foreign policy and many federal, state, and county regulations deny them even the most basic rights. Although hundreds of thousands of them are brothers and sisters in Christ, many of them would not feel welcome in our churches. Allowing them to draw too near might make us aware of their plight and call us to new responsibility, advocacy, compassion, and hospitality. Besides, we might argue, they would surely drain our resources, and they don't have that much to contribute. They are poor; some are uneducated. What might we possibly learn from them?

Churches in the United States are certainly willing to go to these people and their homelands, to get short-term tastes of other worlds, to send missionaries and partner with churches and agencies abroad. It's okay also for our corporations to set up markets in their countries. But this country is our home base; this is our refuge, our secure space! "Surely not, Lord. You would never call us to receive so many immigrants in our midst. If we let too many in, they would affect our language, our culture, our foods . . . They might even change us!" But already, we eat salsa and dance salsa. We are giving immigrants work; they fill our water glasses and wash dishes at the back of our restaurants. We'll let them scrub our kitchens and even care for our children.

If Peter had not accepted Cornelius, none of us Gentiles would be in God's family today. Is it not time for us to welcome today's Corneliuses—the "Corinas" and the "Josés" in our midst—not only to our kitchens and farms, but also to our community and our table?

May we not remain deaf to God's call—repeated, insistent, incessant.

God, re-form our hearts as you did Peter's, so we may open our church and homes to the outsiders you send our way. Amen.

Ruth Padilla DeBorst currently serves as director of spiritual formation and leadership development with World Vision International and as general secretary of the Latin American Theological Fellowship. Ruth has been involved in leadership development and theological education for integral mission in her native Latin America with Christian Reformed World Missions for many years. She and her husband, James, along with their blended, multicultural family, live in Costa Rica.

CHAPTER 5

PREACHING FOR THE
Alternative Community

Whenever I find myself in a discussion with supposedly cutting-edge, culturally keen Christian intellectuals on how church and mission must change in the post-Christendom era, I imagine a group of sixteenth-century Anabaptists in heaven having a good laugh at our expense. "So you've finally figured it out, have you?" I hear them saying with playful pride. "The church can't sleep with the state? You're right, friends—*slow*, but right!"

The Anabaptists and their descendants understood better than anyone else throughout the history of the church that "Christendom"—the unholy marriage of ecclesial and political powers, which wed during the reign of Constantine—was a bad idea. If the postmodern, post-Christendom conversation is right about anything, it is right in pointing out the fact that the marriage between church and state has posed serious problems. Historically, "Anabaptists outraged their contemporaries . . . by their insistence that the Christendom system was fundamentally flawed."[1] In this way, they were "post-Christendom" before the age of post-Christendom.

The Anabaptist vision of *ekklesia* has always included an understanding of the church as the locus of God's reign. As such, the church must stand apart from the world so it can be faithful to its calling—namely, to be the conscience of the powers that be, as well as an alternative to a culture stained with idolatry, immorality, injustice, and violence. The Hutterite leader Eberhard Arnold said it best when he wrote,

> We celebrate the outpouring of the Holy Spirit and the beginning of full community because it meant that Paradise was given back in the midst of an unpeaceful, hostile environment. Jesus had begun this spiritual battle against the injustice of mammon, against impurity in human relationships, and against killing and war. The Church of Jesus Christ is set right into this world to be a place where peace, joy and justice abide, a place of love and unity.[2]

This vision, of course, transcends Anabaptistism, for it is the biblical vision. From the promise of a great nation given to and through Abraham and Sarah (Gen. 12:1-3; 17:15-16) to the formation of the church of "aliens and exiles" in the New Testament (1 Pet. 2:9-11), the call to be the people of God has always meant to be different by demonstrating a higher reality—the kingdom of God. "Everything the church is about . . . hangs on preserving the radical uniqueness of this kingdom in contrast to the kingdom of the world."[3] Contemporary examples of intentional Christian communities shaped by this vision include the Sojourners community in Washington DC, the Jesus People USA in Chicago, the Simple Way in Philadelphia, and the Rutba House in Durham, North Carolina.

This vision of the church as an alternative community constitutes an important dimension of the missional church movement as a whole. The Gospel in Our Culture Network, for example, identifies "taking risks as a contrast community" as a key characteristic of a missional congregation in the United States. "It understands itself as different from the world because of its participation in the life, death, and resurrection of its Lord. It is raising questions, often threatening, about the church's cultural captivity and grappling with the ethical and structural implications of its missional vocation."[4]

The second goal of missional preaching aims to shape the church into the alternative or contrast community God has called it to be. This may sound contradictory to the first goal of inculturation, but it's not; paradoxical, yes, but not contradictory. In fact, together they make up the in-the-world-but-not-of-it spirit of John 17. While inculturation speaks to being *in* the world, the alternative community speaks to not being *of* it. The twin challenges of embracing culture and distinguishing ourselves from it need to be said in one breath if we are to grasp the creative tension of the biblical relationship between church and world.

A Peculiar People

Both Paul and Peter called the church what the King James Version translates as "a peculiar people" (Tit. 2:14 and 1 Pet. 2:9). This is not being peculiar for peculiar's sake, as if God intends us to be snooty nonconformists. Rather, from the beginning the church has been called to be a positively different kind of people with a fundamentally different agenda than the rest of the world. To be peculiar is what John Howard Yoder calls "the original revolution, the creation of a distinct community with its own deviant set of rules."[5]

However, in order to be revolutionary in society as the alternative community of Christ, the church cannot allow itself to devolve into a marginalized sect that the rest of the world can easily ignore or dismiss. Here is where inculturation, which calls for full participation in culture, and the alternative community properly intersect. We are called to be different, but because we are fully engaged in mainstream life, the larger community cannot ignore us; or to say it more positively, the larger community views us as relevant to the rest of the culture.

Subculture or Counterculture?

What the church has to say, however, more often than not challenges the very core of the larger culture. By virtue of its alternative nature, the church serves as prophetic conscience and moral compass of society. In this sense the church must go beyond being a mere subculture and become more a counterculture. Howard Snyder's comments on this distinction are helpful here. He explains that the church as subculture is "in fundamental agreement with the dominant culture on major issues and values, but has distinct secondary values and characteristics."[6] As a subculture, the church may have its own pop culture (I think of contemporary Christian music and "Left Behind" novels, for example) and may engage in activities peculiar to its members (such as Sunday worship, Vacation Bible School, etc.), but it fundamentally aligns with society's core values on politics, education, and lifestyle.

By contrast, the church as counterculture is "in tension with the dominant culture at the level of fundamental values, even though it may share many secondary characteristics with that culture."[7] For example, the people of God may line up with the rest of culture in their artistic and entertainment preferences (secondary characteristics), while being fundamentally at odds with the consumerism, middle-classism, and militarism that constitute the heart of American society. In one of his early books, social activist Jim Wallis asserted, "God's call to discipleship, the call to follow Jesus Christ, demands a fundamental break with the dominant values and conformist patterns of the majority culture."[8] God's call upon the church to be the alternative community is not the formation of a subculture, but of a counterculture.

Stanley Hauerwas and Will Willimon have another term to describe God's peculiar, countercultural people. They write, "In baptism our citizenship is transferred from one dominion to another, and we become, in whatever culture we find ourselves, *resident aliens*."[9] This description does well to acknowledge that although we live here, we must keep our alien status, for our primary citizenship lies elsewhere now and forevermore—the kingdom of heaven (Phil. 3:20).

Alternative Community as Mission

Being the alternative community—a peculiar, countercultural people—sets the foundation for the church's mission in the world; indeed, this itself is the beginning of mission. That is, world mission begins by the church demonstrating love, peace, justice, and reconciliation within its own walls. In the words of Jesus, "By this everyone will know that you are my disciples, if you have love for one another" (John 13:35). The alternative community demonstrates that the message of the kingdom of God works in real life.

By *being* the church, we present an inherent invitation to onlookers that says something like, "Do you like what you see? Come and join us." The church, then, as a demonstration of the kingdom, attracts the wayward, the tired, the poor, the oppressed, the marginalized, and others who long for redemption from the pains and struggles of this life, inviting them to become a part of the peculiar people of God. In this way, the alternative community, the church, is itself mission.

As the church grows in its ability to demonstrate kingdom life among its members, it can then engage the world together in proactive mission, extending God's goodness to the ends of the earth.

As the alternative community, we spread the love, peace, and justice of the kingdom until these kingdom realities engulf all of existence. Indeed "the formation of the people of God—where the redeemed enjoy justice, equality, peace, righteousness, and joy—was intended to model nothing less than the new humanity."[10]

Characteristics of Alternative People

We who make up God's alternative community are called to affirm certain truths and display certain behaviors.

Worship as Allegiance

Above all else, we worship the God of the universe, revealed most fully in Jesus Christ, and by doing so, pledge primary allegiance to the kingdom of God. We see anything less as false worship, as idolatry. Contrary to popular notions, idolatry is not limited to voodoo dolls and totem poles in faraway lands; indeed every culture has its idols, which demand absolute allegiance. Marva Dawn identifies several main idols that threaten the North American church, including the gods of efficiency, money, tradition, and success.[11] The church is an alternative community in that it sees these things as lesser gods and refuses to bow down to them, even if all others do. Members of the alternative community have the audacity to claim to know the God of the universe in the person of Jesus Christ, and it is this God whom alternative people worship.

A Biblical People

Members of the alternative community look to the Bible as the final authority for faith and practice. We are people of the Book, believing that Scripture is the most reliable source of God's saving activity in the world. "Let us remind ourselves," write Sider and his colleagues, "that we are people shaped by the living Word as it is revealed in the written Word—people who meditate on the Bible's magnificent stories, who sing its songs, and who internalize its truths, believing that through the words of Scripture we hear God's guiding voice for today."[12]

In fact, it is by heeding the voice of the living God through the pages of Scripture, and not the voices of Hollywood, pop psychology, political leaders, or the religious establishment, that we become the alternative community. Only "a new biblical radicalism can provide the basis for people willing to have their own lives changed, to challenge the system, and to provide alternative vision."[13] Insofar as we are truly and radically biblical people, we become the countercultural community of disciples that we are called to be.

Peace, Justice, and Reconciliation

Alternative people also strive to be reconciled in peace with one another across lines of gender, race, and socioeconomic status. In taking the Sermon on the Mount seriously, we strive to love our enemies.[14] One distinguishing mark of the alternative community is its effort to model reconciliation among its members. I will say more about this in Chapter 7. Suffice it to say here that the church's commitment to peace, justice, and reconciliation flies in the face of a culture characterized by divisions, injustice, and retaliation.

Furthermore, we are called to hold our material goods loosely, and not to privilege the wealthy in the community. We are to be driven by the vision of having no poor among us, as we practice the "economic *koinonia*" of the early church, where God's people shared possessions with one another and no favoritism existed.[15] "Over and over God commanded his people to live together in community in such a way that all families would have the resources to earn a decent livelihood and that those who could not care for themselves would be generously taken care of."[16] Such "holistic fellowship" goes against the grain of the highly individualized and privatized economics of today's culture.

Preaching for the Alternative Community

I have painted quite an idealistic picture of the church, of how it is *supposed* to be. But anyone who has been part of congregational life for any length of time knows all too well how marred this picture can get in the nitty-gritty of life together. The redeemed-but-still-imperfect body of Christ all too often does not love, does not show compassion, and does not do justice. This only highlights the importance of continuing, in grace and love, to uphold the church's call to love one another in peace and justice in our preaching and teaching.

Preaching that is missional aims to strengthen the truth of our kingdom citizenship, our status as resident aliens, our peculiarity. By preaching for the alternative community, we help the church become the demonstration of right-side-up living, which testifies to the Reign of God in and for the world. There are at least three guiding principles for preaching for the alternative community.

In the World but Not of It

We preach to equip God's people to be countercultural while still being fully immersed in the surrounding culture. There are several reasons the church must embrace the world in all its brokenness. First, we seek to extend God's love to the world because we are still a part of this world. So by extending love and grace to the world, we extend these things to ourselves. And second, because "God so loved the world that he gave his only Son, so that everyone who believes in him may not perish but may have eternal life" (John 3:16). In light of the experience of redemption found in Jesus Christ, the church's embrace of the world must reflect not only the unconditional love of God (inculturation) but also the transforming love of God (alternative community). A reviewer in *The Toronto Star* of Hauerwas and Willimon's *Resident Aliens* captures this paradox well when he writes, "The authors . . . do not call on the church to become an exclusive sect which gathers in self-righteous judgment on the world. Rather they call on the church to become what it was originally—'a colony of heaven,' a colony that challenges a world it *loves* and is willing to die for but not conform to."[17] We preach "the otherness of the church"[18] for the sake of a world that we know and love.

Kingdom Politics

We preach a nonpartisan agenda with regard to the social issues of our times, transcending the categories of left and right. Or, more positively, we preach the kingdom of God; we preach nothing less than the gospel! As the church, we are political by nature, but we are an alternative *polis* and should preach accordingly. Contrary to the misguided notion that we need to avoid tough social questions (an accusation often made against alternative community advocates), we do not shy away from preaching about the issues that impact contemporary society. Society needs to hear from the alternative *polis* called the church regarding education, poverty, family, abortion, sexuality, war, and so on—as long as the church's contribution remains faithful to the unique message of the kingdom.

It is when its proclamation sounds consistently like the agenda of a particular political party that the church gets into trouble; for when this begins to happen, it has likely become ideologically captive and therefore uninteresting and irrelevant, even idolatrous. With primarily right-wing evangelicals in America in mind, Gregory Boyd, in his now famous (or "infamous," depending on your point of view) *The Myth of a Christian Nation,* charges, "a significant segment of American evangelicalism is guilty of nationalistic and political idolatry."[19] Although Boyd lists his reasons for focusing on Christians who have been co-opted by the right, he makes it clear that his "thesis applies as much to Christians on the political left."[20] To preach the authentic alternative community means to remain faithful to the kingdom vision of society, which requires remaining free from the powerful allure of political ideologies.

A Martyr's Faith

We also preach to remain faithful unto death. Despite all the sugarcoating we may want to apply, preaching for the alternative community ultimately must call for a martyr's faith. It stands to reason, insofar as the church challenges the status quo and threatens the political and economic power structures, that it will encounter hostility. It is in this ultimately hostile environment that the alternative community called the church must take a stand to reflect the righteousness, peace, mercy, and justice of God at all costs. More often than not, however, such a stance results in suffering; for the world has historically lashed out against truth-tellers and all who refuse to bow down before human thrones.

Disciples of Jesus understand this in light of the fact that the world hung their Lord on a cross. As Yoder avers, "The cross is to be understood . . . as that kind of suffering that comes upon one because of loyalty to Jesus and nonconformity to the world."[21] In this light, preaching for the alternative community calls disciples to inevitable suffering. "It is no accident," Yoder continues, "that the word 'martyr' has the double meaning of testimony and innocent suffering. The suffering of the church . . . is according to both Scripture and experience the continuing destiny of any faithful Christian community."[22]

■ ■ ■

Pastor Gregory Boyd's sermon "My Kingdom Is Not of This World" is a powerful example of a message that is undergirded by the notion of the church as an alternative community. How does it question our national allegiance and call us back to our first love? How does it challenge us to be different from prevailing culture, or more positively, how does it urge us to be loyal to the kingdom of God?

NOTES

1. Stuart Murray Williams, "A Voice from the Past—Anabaptism, Spirituality and Social Justice," in *Following Fire: How the Spirit Leads Us to Fight Injustice*, ed. Cheryl Catford (Springvale, Vic, Australia: Urban Neighbors of Hope, 2008), 187.
2. Eberhard Arnold, "Church," in *God's Revolution*, eds. Hutterian Society of Brothers and John Howard Yoder (New York: Paulist, 1984), 52.
3. Gregory A. Boyd, *The Myth of a Christian Nation: How the Quest for Political Power is Destroying the Church* (Grand Rapids: Zondervan, 2005), 14.
4. Lois Y. Barrett et al., *Treasure in Clay Jars: Patterns in Missional Faithfulness* (Grand Rapids: Eerdmans, 2004), 74.
5. John Howard Yoder, *The Original Revolution: Essays on Christian Pacifism* (Scottdale, PA: Herald, 1971), 28.
6. Howard Snyder, *Liberating the Church: The Ecology of Church & Kingdom* (Downers Grove: IVP, 1983), 120.
7. Snyder, *Liberating the Church*, 120.
8. Jim Wallis, *Agenda for Biblical People* (New York: Harper & Row, 1976), 11.
9. Stanley Hauerwas and William H. Willimon, *Resident Aliens* (Nashville: Abingdon, 1989), 12.
10. Ronald J. Sider, John M. Perkins, Wayne L. Gordon, and F. Albert Tizon, *Linking Arms, Linking Lives: How Urban-Suburban Partnerships Can Transform Communities* (Grand Rapids: Baker, 2008), 44.
11. Marva Dawn, *Reaching Out without Dumbing Down: A Theology of Worship for the Turn of the Century Church* (Grand Rapids: Eerdmans, 1995), 42–53.
12. Sider et al., *Linking Arms, Linking Lives*, 41.
13. Wallis, *Agenda for Biblical People*, 10.
14. I love what Williams says about Anabaptists in "A Voice from the Past." In describing their distinctions, he writes, "They insisted that the Sermon on the Mount and other teachings of Jesus were to be obeyed rather than admired" (180).
15. Ronald J. Sider, *Rich Christians in an Age of Hunger: Moving From Affluence to Generosity*, 5th ed. (Dallas: Word, 2005), 81–88.
16. Sider, *Rich Christians*, 85–86.
17. Quoted in Stanley Hauerwas and William H. Willimon, *Where Residents Aliens Live* (Nashville: Abingdon, 1996), 99.

18. This is the title of one of John Howard Yoder's better-known essays, which can be found in various places, including *The Royal Priesthood*, ed. Michael G. Cartwright (Grand Rapids: Eerdmans, 1994), 53–64.

19. Boyd, *The Myth of a Christian Nation*, 11.

20. Boyd, *The Myth of a Christian Nation*, 14.

21. John Howard Yoder, "A People in the World," in *The Royal Priesthood*, ed. Michael G. Cartwright (Grand Rapids: Eerdmans, 1994), 87.

22. John Howard Yoder, "A People in the World," 86.

My Kingdom Is Not of This World

■ ■ ■

Gregory A. Boyd
JOHN 18:36

Politics was in the air. For several centuries, the Jews had been under Roman or Greek oppression, and they were tired of it—not just because their rights were being denied, but also because they were the alleged people who worshiped the one true God, and yet these pagans had authority over them. And they took that as a slam not only against them but against their God. It was in this context that Jesus came.

In that world, everything Jesus did was politically significant. People tried to pull him into their political agendas, and what's amazing is that Jesus never allowed himself to be co-opted. That very fact was a huge political statement because he was saying that the kingdom he had come to bring is not of this world. He didn't play by the rules of this world; he didn't buy into the agendas and the conflicts and the polarities and the struggles of the kingdoms of this world. He came to build a countercultural kingdom—a kingdom that operates by a totally different methodology. He could have done what a lot of people wanted him to do—overthrow the Roman government. He could have called ten thousand legions of angels. He could have done that. Instead he allowed himself to be crucified by the kingdom of the world. Why? In order to establish the kingdom that is of God.

And now his people are called to imitate him. He *was* the kingdom of God here on earth, and now the kingdom of God is to be present in all who follow him. The very choice of his disciples points to one way in which God's kingdom, which Jesus came to build, was unique. On the one hand, he chose Simon the Zealot, a member of a Jewish sect that despised the Roman government enough to take up arms trying to overthrow it. On the other hand he chose Matthew, a tax collector, a Jew who worked for the Roman government to collect taxes from its subjects.

So let's get this straight: Jesus called Simon the Zealot, despiser of tax collectors, and then he also called Matthew the tax collector. He said, "Follow me," to both. I don't think we have categories to describe how radically different a Simon and a Matthew would be today. To say Matthew was a sort of right-wing Rush Limbaugh and Simon a kind of left-wing Ralph Nader still wouldn't quite capture the gulf between these two. If you were to say a Rush Limbaugh and a communist you'd be getting closer to the gulf between Simon and Matthew; and yet Jesus called them both to be part of the kingdom of God. I'm sure Matthew and Simon had some very interesting discussions around the campfire at night.

What is absolutely mind-boggling is that never once in the Gospels do we read of Jesus commenting on these very different approaches to the government of their day. And his silence on the matter speaks volumes about the kingdom of God—namely, that it's radically different than the kingdoms of this world. What Jesus showed was this: When we claim him as our Lord and Savior, and we are part of a kingdom that is centered on him, then what we have in common dwarfs our differences in terms of our political orientation. If we're really thinking along the lines of the kingdom of God, then I should be able to get up here and tell you I love Rush Limbaugh and that shouldn't bother you. You shouldn't question my faith. Or if I told you I'm a card-carrying socialist; that shouldn't cause you to question my salvation. Because our faith does not hinge on our philosophies about how government should be run. It *does* hinge on our common and primary allegiance to Jesus Christ and the radically, unique kind of kingdom he calls us all into. His kingdom is not of this world.

There are two kingdoms, and everything hangs on our keeping them distinct. There's the kingdom of the world, and there's the kingdom of God. I hear language in the church today that concerns me—

this concept that we need to take America back for God. Back to what? The assumption behind this language is that once upon a time America was a Christian nation. I want to submit to you that *Christian nation* is a contradiction in terms. When we fuse them, as many of us have, it yields disastrous consequences. It harms our witness of God's love in the world.

John 13:35 says, "Your love for one another will prove to the world that you are my disciples" (NLT). In John 17:21 Jesus prayed, "I pray that they will all be one, just as you and I are one . . . so that the world will believe you sent me" (NLT)—paraphrased, "I pray that they would embody the love of the triune God, that perfect, unsurpassable, unconditional love that characterizes God throughout eternity." Why? So that all creation can experience that love. As the church manifests Calvary-like love to all people at all times in all situations, no "ifs, ands, or buts," the world sees Jesus Christ and gets a glimpse of the kingdom of God. That's what Jesus prayed in John 17. As Simon and Matthew love each other, the world sees a love it is not capable of; it sees a kingdom that is not of this world.

But if we identify the United States (or any other country) as a Christian nation then Caesar gets entangled in the word *Christian*. Whatever our nation does is understood as Christian. Now, America does a lot of good things, but it also sometimes does some nasty things. Does the church want to identify with all of it? I contend that we shouldn't identify with any of it! When we identify a nation as Christian, everything the nation does weakens our distinct, unique witness of love in the world.

It is to the advantage of the kingdom of God to say as loudly and clearly as we can, "God's kingdom is not of this world," and "America is not the kingdom of God!" And China is not the kingdom of God, and the Soviet Union is not the kingdom of God, nor is any other human kingdom. The kingdom of God is manifest wherever people are willing to lay down their lives for others and serve others and turn the other cheek and do those radically foolish things that characterize the kingdom of God. The kingdom of God happens when people imitate Jesus, not Caesar. We've got to keep the two kingdoms distinct. And the idea of a "Christian nation" undermines that.

The fusing of the kingdom of God and the kingdom of the world undermines the mission focus of the church. If you go to Cambodia as a missionary it's not hard to stay focused, because everything around you reminds you that you're an alien there. You're not first and foremost a citizen of Cambodia. Your alien status in that predominantly Buddhist country reminds you that you're there to communicate in word and deed the truth of Jesus Christ's lordship, demonstrate God's outlandish love, and win people's hearts over to Jesus Christ. I'm sure being a missionary in Cambodia has its hardships, but at least it's clear. It's precisely that clarity that's lacking here in the United States because the majority of people here say they're Christians. Polls show that over 80 percent of Americans identify themselves as Christian; however, by any sort of biblical definition of Christianity, that self-designation means very little. Basically, it means, "Well, I'm born in America, and this is a Christian nation, and I'm a pretty decent person."

What we've got here (and I believe it's what we've always had here) is a form of Deism, a belief in some impersonal god that may have some social value, but that's it. At best, it's a veneer of Christianity. We've got a semblance, a sort of quasi-Christian cloaking on everything. What we've got here is a civil religion where there are principles and echoes of Christianity. We have "one nation under God" in our pledge, and we've got "in God we trust" on our currency, and we say a blessing before a meal, and we say a prayer before football games and other social functions (at least in some places). We've got a social sort of religion going on.

But look beneath the surface, look past the "in God we trust," and what you will find is something that is altogether pagan. And I submit to you that, if you pull back this veneer of the social civil religion, America is a pagan nation. It is not any better or any worse than any other nation. America needs kingdom missionaries just as much as Buddhist Cambodia.

There was a student I met at Bethel College who'd grown up on a farm in South Dakota. He was a sculptor. He shared with me that one thing he used to do in his spare time was to take some manure—cow dung—and sculpt it into things. Manure art! Kind of gross, but that's what he did. He would take cow dung and fashion it into shapes of people or flowers or whatever, and then he would put a certain kind of veneer on it to harden it. Then he would paint it and make it look like a porcelain doll or something! But, you see, it was still manure.

Now if we can see that the manure stands for everything that's inconsistent with the kingdom of God, then what we have here in America is a civil religion that serves as a nice veneer on manure. All the polish and the veneer and the painting in the world—the laws, the customs, the traditions, whatever—doesn't make manure any less manure.

The only thing that can begin to "transform manure" is the Spirit of God. I was a pile of dung, but God has taken this pile of dung and he breathed life into it. He made it a new creature in Christ Jesus. God said, "Greg Boyd, your heart is a pile of dung; let me work with it." And the way God has worked with it is through Calvary-like love where Jesus has begun to change the way I think about myself, the way I feel about God, the way I feel about other people. And now there's life coming into this dung, although there is still dung behavior that needs changing. In Christ, I'm a new creature, and so is everybody who puts faith in Jesus Christ.

Only God can take a sinner and turn him or her into a saint. You can pass a law to keep a racist from committing racial acts, but only God can take the racism out of that person. You can pass laws that keep a person from stealing, but only God can take away the desire to steal. Only God can change the heart. Only God can change the mind. Only God can change a nation. And God does it on the inside—by looking past, going past, and working past the external veneer.

Our unique role as kingdom people is to see through the veneer. If we think we are in a Christian nation, if we buy the veneer, then we'll end up spending a whole lot of time and energy trying to polish up the veneer. And we'll think that if we just make it a little shinier and a little brighter and form it this way or that way then it will be less manure-like. If we buy into the veneer, then we lose our mission focus. We pollute the distinct missionary call on our lives. In fact, we talk about missionaries as those who go to other countries, because we don't see the need for missionaries here. And worse, we don't see ourselves as missionaries. I'm here to tell you that the United States needs missionaries—and that we are those missionaries! It's just that the need is a little more difficult to see sometimes because there's that quasi-Christian sort of veneer around, which convinces people they are already right with God.

Now, if you're asked your opinion about the veneer—give it. That's fine. Be a Matthew or a Simon; I don't care. But never forget that the veneer is just a veneer. And what we're called to do primarily is to provide an opportunity for God to work on the inside, on the dung itself. Church, let us keep our focus. Let us not buy into the veneer. Paul says this in 2 Timothy 2:4, "Soldiers don't get tied up in the affairs of civilian life, for then they cannot please the officer who enlisted them" (NLT). The image Paul uses is of a Roman soldier stationed in a foreign land. Paul is saying that a good soldier knows better than to get overly entangled in civilian affairs, which would distract him (or her).

Our main vision is to love everyone, everywhere, at all times; to sacrifice our lives, patterned after the cross of Calvary, for their sake, because God loves each and every person. It's through our mustard seed love that this radical, alternative, very different, peculiar reality called the kingdom of God is going to grow.

Gregory A. Boyd is founder and senior pastor of Woodland Hills Church in St. Paul, Minnesota, and founder and president of Christus Victor Ministries. Greg is a national and international speaker at churches, colleges, conferences, and retreats, and has appeared on numerous radio and television shows. He has authored or co-authored eighteen books, including the bestselling *The Myth of a Christian Nation.*

CHAPTER 6

PREACHING FOR
Holistic
Transformation

The mission committee recently realized that beyond donating canned goods to the local food bank on a quarterly basis, we really don't have anything resembling a theology of compassion and justice. We are almost exclusively evangelistic in orientation, but we want to grow in our social awareness and involvement. Can you help us? —Mission Committee of First Evangelical Church

Let me get right to the point: We have not done evangelism in years, maybe ever. We have no problem with social action, as our ministries to the homeless and the socially-marginalized demonstrate. But I confess that "evangelism" is a put-off to many of our members. I believe our church needs a fresh understanding of what it means to share the gospel. Can you help us? —Pastor Jane, Mainline Church USA

The above emails typify what I find in my inbox as director of Word & Deed Network, a ministry that seeks to help local congregations grow in holistic community engagement. Thankfully, the evangelism versus social concern debate no longer rages as intensely as it once did. Ron Sider writes, "Fifty years ago the generalizations that evangelical Christians do evangelism and liberal Christians do social action was largely accurate. Today that is no longer even close to matching reality. At least in more and more evangelical congregations, denominations and para-church ministries, holistic ministry is the norm."[1] Sider and other courageous evangelicals in the 1970s and '80s fought relentlessly on the front lines of this battle, and in the words of one of them, "We won!"[2]

While we should celebrate this "victory," we must also acknowledge the thoroughgoing, long-lasting damage done by the battle. The poison of dichotomous thinking regarding evangelism and social concern has seeped into the church's bloodstream, resulting in a chronic struggle for ministry balance. Consequently, many Christians today still have trouble grasping the holistic nature of the gospel, and many churches continue to demonstrate lopsidedness in their practical outreach. While some congregations focus on the personal, individual level (evangelism, discipleship, etc.), others focus on the corporate, societal level (compassion ministries, public policy, justice, etc.). So, even though increasing numbers of congregations affirm holistic ministry in principle, there are still relatively few that do both evangelism and social concern effectively on the practical level.

Given this reality, I cannot stress enough the importance of preaching that proclaims the wholeness of the gospel. Preaching for holistic transformation—i.e., preaching the good news of Christ that redeems every aspect of our existence—is an integral part of the long-term healing of the church and the redemption of the world.

Toward a Holistic Theology

I believe we need a theology of holistic transformation to undergird our holistic proclamation. This theology is built on at least two assumptions.

The Human Being: A Body-Soul Unity in Community

The first assumption concerns our understanding of the essence of the human being. If, for example, we define the human being as a soul that is temporarily housed in flesh but destined for an immaterial, disembodied reality called heaven (or hell), then the soul holds prominence over the body. And, "if the soul is the most important aspect . . . then presumably, 'spiritual' things are vastly more important than 'physical' or 'secular' concerns."[3] To "save souls" from an irredeemable, temporal, material world becomes the primary, if not the sole, definition of mission. In this view, flesh and blood fall pathetically short of the glory of God; the body is, in fact, hopelessly evil and destined for decay, and we should be happy that someday we will shed this mortal coil.

How does this view of the human being square up with Scripture? It doesn't! In fact, it bears the marks of a heresy that refuses to go away: Gnosticism. Among other misguided beliefs, the Christian version of Gnosticism rejects the notion that God took on real flesh in Jesus Christ. If Christ took on real flesh and blood, yet flesh is ultimately evil, then that means Christ took on evil. And if Christ took on evil, then he was in no position to save the world; for how can evil redeem evil? Redemption in the Gnostic Christ (who only *appears* human) is in fact liberation from the prison cell of the flesh and union with Christ in pure, spiritual bliss.

Gnosticism remains alarmingly ubiquitous among Bible-believing Christians. In response to a question regarding this, celebrated theologian N. T. Wright said, "There is this idea that the world is just really so much rubbish; this is just a silly old world; God is going to throw it in the trash can. We're going to be raptured up to heaven and then there will be a great Armageddon, and the sooner the better."[4] But is not the world that God made, including and especially humanity, deemed good by its own Creator (Gen. 1:31)?

If the Bible teaches us that the created world is good, what does it say concerning the nature of the human person? God's desire to redeem all of creation (Rom. 8:22-25), the fact that God took on flesh in the person of Jesus Christ (John 1:14), the promise of the glorious resurrection of the body of which Christ's was the first fruit (1 Cor. 15:35-58), the positive body metaphors for the church (1 Cor. 4:14-16), and apostolic teachings that specifically counter the heresy that Christ did not come in the flesh (1 John 4:1-6) all point to the human person as wholly and wonderfully made. The human being is a "body-soul unity"; that is, "the spirit, the body, the mind, and the emotions are all part of what it means to be created in the image of God, together making up the total human being."[5] As such, no aspect of human existence takes precedence over another.

Furthermore, the human being is a "body-soul unity in community," that is, a physical-spiritual being that by its very nature requires other physical-spiritual beings in order to be whole.[6] This means the social dimension of human existence is also integral to the church's mission. In this view, the physical, spiritual, and *social* aspects make up the human person. We cannot reduce mission to ministering to one part of the human person at the expense of other parts. No missional activity is superior to another. Quoting Wright once again:

> Every act of love, gratitude, and kindness; every work of art or music inspired by . . . [God's] creation; . . . every act of care and nurture, of comfort and support for one's fellow human beings and for that matter, one's fellow nonhuman creatures; and of course . . . every deed that spreads the gospel, builds up the church, . . . and makes the name of Jesus honored in the world—all of this will find its way, through the resurrecting power of God, into the new creation that God will one day make. That is the logic of the mission of God.[7]

A Case for Holistic Ministry

When we speak then of transformation—because indeed, the human condition is in need of God's transforming touch—we must have the whole of the human being in view. As such, the church does not have the option to work on the personal transformational level—personal evangelism, personal growth, the cultivation of the inner life, healing, etc.—without working on the social transformational level—responsible citizenry, justice, peace, advocacy, public policy, etc. And the reverse is equally true: it cannot work on social transformation without also working on the personal matters of the heart. The whole thing—creation, society, and every aspect of every person—needs to change! The whole thing needs God's healing, transforming touch. This is the second assumption upon which a theology of holistic transformation is built.

The thoroughness of human need hit me hard during a field-based graduate level course I took in the mid-1980s. Visiting three Central American countries over a period of three weeks, I saw with my own eyes the misery and suffering of so many people whom God loved. The visceral experience of being with the poor by day, and doing the required readings on a theology of poverty by night, changed me profoundly. "Saving souls" without taking physical need and the social situation seriously made less and less sense; in fact, it sounded more and more ridiculous by the end of the course. I became convinced that if the gospel did not address the full gamut of human need, which I saw and smelled and felt among the poor, then the good news was no good at all. That course changed me at the core, which is why I refer to it today as my "born again *again*" experience.

This led me to almost a decade of mission work among the poor in the Philippines, which only reinforced my belief in the absolute need for a holistic approach to mission. In fact, I am convinced that it's only when missional reflection is separated from the nitty-gritty of the practice of ministry that the artificial question arises, "Which is more important—the spiritual or the social, word or deed, evangelism or justice?" Holistic need calls for holistic ministry.

Holistic ministry is the practice of God's people that is based on the full implications of the gospel of the kingdom, believing the good news of Jesus Christ is salvation for the whole person—body, mind, spirit, and social relationships—and for the whole of existence—creation, nations, and sociopolitical structures—proclaiming the gospel by both word and deed for the sake of all, especially the poor. Preaching for holistic transformation does its part in moving the church toward fulfilling the richness of this definition. It affirms the inseparability of the personal and the social as it aspires to generate, by God's word, transformation on all levels, from the human heart to sociopolitical structures to the cosmos.

Characteristics of a Holistic Congregation

As we preach the whole gospel week after week, month after month, and year after year, our congregations should begin reflecting certain characteristics.[8]

Holistic Worship

First, we begin to understand that God cares not just for the spiritual realm, but for all realms of human existence. And to worship a holistic God cannot but result in a community of holistically minded disciples. We become more holistic as we gain a clearer understanding of God's comprehensive agenda for the world. As Sider, Olson, and Unruh write,

> When we dedicate ourselves to the God "who forgiveth all thine iniquities; who healeth all thy diseases; who redeemeth thy life from destruction; who crowneth thee with lovingkindness and tender mercies; who satisfieth thy mouth with good things" (Ps. 103:3-5,

KJV), we thereby dedicate ourselves to proclaiming God's forgiveness, healing diseases, showing mercy, and filling the mouths of the hungry.[9]

Holistic Care for One Another

A second characteristic of a holistic congregation is that its members take care of one another holistically. Inspired by biblical passages such as Acts 2:44, where "All who believed were together and had all things in common; they would sell their possessions and goods and distribute the proceeds to all, as any had need," we are not just concerned about our spiritual lives but for one another's entire well-being. Such a commitment usually manifests in a robust benevolence ministry or a strong group of deacons attuned to the needs of the congregation. A holistic congregation understands the importance of demonstrating among its members the compassion and justice it desires for the community at large (Gal. 6:10).

Holistic Concern for Community Transformation

Third, we view the whole community (and world) as God's domain. We know that God's blessings are not exclusive to us; they are not reserved for the church. God's blessings need to flow out from the church and into the streets of the community. A holistic congregation has recovered the idea of the parish. "A parish differs from a congregation," writes Eric Swanson, "in that it is a geographical scope of concern and responsibility. A congregation is a subset of a parish."[10] What would happen if our congregations began to take responsibility for our respective communities, instead of just our own members? Whether we use the term or not, a parish view of ministry has helped holistically minded congregations justify involvement in community transformation.

Concrete Holistic Action

And fourth, we *practice* holistic ministry; that is, we take pains to be concrete, to take action. A church that has been soaked in holistic preaching and teaching will get easily frustrated if its leaders merely talk about holistic ministry. Members will become increasingly restless, longing to be "doers of the word and not merely hearers" (Jas. 1:22). To say it more positively, a congregation of holistically minded disciples will be energized to engage in transformational activities, for it knows that "religion that is pure and undefiled before God, the Father, is this: to care for orphans and widows in their distress, and to keep oneself unstained by the world" (Jas. 1:27).

Preaching for Holistic Transformation

Several key preaching themes emerge as we begin to take seriously the truth and practice of holistic transformation.

Integrity of the Human Person

Fundamentally, we preach the integrity of the human person; that is, we keep all the dimensions of the human being integral and intact. We are not souls trapped in a fleshly prison, tolerating society, culture, and politics until Christ returns; nor are we mere biological entities, making the best of our situation until we turn back to dust.[11] We were created as body-soul unities in community, and we will be redeemed in the same way. Preaching that leads to a holistic understanding of mission keeps the integrity of the human person in full view.

Furthermore, we present the future of God (heaven) as fully material, touchable, and visible. Heaven is ultimate *real*-ity. As Tom Sine has written, heaven will be more than "clouds, harps, and angel wings!"[12] We will, as fully embodied and redeemed persons, occupy the new heavens and the new earth in unimaginable, blissful union with the Trinitarian God and with one another.

Preaching this full-bodied eschatological view of the human future has implications for mission today, for as Wright so eloquently expresses, "A proper grasp of the *future* hope held out to us in Jesus Christ leads directly . . . to a vision of *present* hope that is the basis of all Christian mission."[13] Jesus put it even more simply and poetically: "Your kingdom come. Your will be done, on earth as it is in heaven" (Matt. 6:10).

Human Brokenness and Kingdom Transformation

We also preach the two-pronged message of human fallibility and kingdom transformation. A holistic view of humanity does not mean that we are whole in the sense that nothing at all is wrong with us. Indeed, there is something *very* wrong with us, along with the whole of the universe. Since the mishap in the Garden, we have alienated ourselves from God and one another. We hate and kill. We care only for ourselves, and turn a blind eye to the plight of our neighbors. We don't love our spouses and then covet other people's spouses. We cheat. We lie. We carelessly trample upon the planet. Need I go on? The Scriptures affirm the holistic constitution of the human person; but almost in the same breath, they also lament the utter brokenness of the human person—and of all creation.

But even as holistic preaching does not hold back in declaring the depth of our brokenness, it also celebrates healing and redemption in Jesus Christ for all of creation and for all who believe. "Who will separate us from the love of Christ?" asked the apostle Paul. "Will hardship, or distress, or persecution, or famine, or nakedness, or peril, or sword? . . . No, in all these things we are more than conquerors through him who loved us" (Rom. 8:35-37). Preaching for holistic transformation feels the depth and completeness of human brokenness, and celebrates God's redemptive plan in Jesus Christ.

Unity of Evangelism, Compassion, and Justice

Finally, we preach the unity of evangelism, compassion, and justice. This certainly does not mean we never preach a sermon that is just about evangelism or just about social concern. To be sure, there are appropriate times to focus primarily on evangelism or to give special attention to social concerns in our preaching. For example, during the 2008 presidential elections, when an African American man and a white woman were on the tickets of their respective parties, many church leaders felt led to focus sermons on either the relationship between faith and politics, or to offer kingdom thinking regarding the chronic social problems of racism and sexism. But even when specific situations urge us to highlight a specific part of the gospel message, we should always do so with the awareness of the other side of the coin. Evangelism, compassion, and justice are all essential elements in the unified holistic gospel that must pervade our preaching.

■ ■ ■

In "Is Our Church Growing—God-Style?" church consultant Heidi Rolland Unruh unpacks Paul's letter to the Ephesians and derives from it trajectories of true church growth, i.e., toward holistic transformation. How does the sermon call us to personal growth? How does it invite us to grow in ministries of evangelism, compassion and justice for the sake of social transformation?

NOTES

1. Ronald J. Sider, in the Foreword of Al Tizon, *Transformation after Lausanne* (Oxford et al.: Regnum; Eugene, OR: Wipf & Stock, 2008), viii.
2. For a more detailed treatment of this battle that raged within the evangelical missionary community, see my volume, *Transformation after Lausanne*, 17–97.
3. Ronald J. Sider, *Good News and Good Works* (Grand Rapids: Baker, 2007), 30.
4. "Let's Try to Keep the China on the Table: Homiletics Interview with N. T. Wright," in *Homiletics Online*, October 2006. http://www.homileticsonline.com/subscriber/interviews/wright.asp (accessed August 9, 2010).
5. Ronald J. Sider, Philip N. Olson, and Heidi Rolland Unruh, *Churches That Make a Difference* (Grand Rapids: Baker, 2002), 49.
6. Sider et al., *Churches That Make a Difference*, 49–50.
7. N. T. Wright, *Surprised by Hope: Rethinking Heaven, the Resurrection, and the Mission of the Church* (New York: HarperOne, 2008), 208.
8. These characteristics are loosely based upon a summary of principles found originally in Sider et al., *Churches That Make a Difference*, but found in summary form as "Tool #6: Qualities of Holistic Congregations" in Heidi Unruh and Phil Olson, *Becoming a Church That Makes a Difference DVD* (Wynnewood, PA: Evangelicals for Social Action, 2006).
9. Sider et al., *Churches That Make a Difference*, 131.
10. Eric Swanson, "Ten Paradigm Shifts Toward Community Transformation," *Leadership Network* (2003), 11. http://www.leadnet.org/downloads/TenShifts.pdf (accessed August 9, 2010).
11. Sider et al., *Churches That Make a Difference*, 48–49.
12. Tom Sine, *Why Settle for More and Miss the Best?* (Waco: Word, 1987), 40.
13. Wright, *Surprised by Hope*, 191.

Is Our Church Growing—God-Style?

■ ■ ■

Heidi Rolland Unruh
LETTER TO EPHESIANS

A number of years ago I helped teach a seminary class called Growing Holistic Congregations. I will never forget the questions raised by one of the students in a reflection paper. She wrote:

What makes the difference? Why is one church a place of total transformation, while another is a place where people are saved and then sit there until they die? What kind of church changes the community and what kind of church is just there taking up space, with members who are not challenged and not growing? . . . What I am looking for is renewal- and action-driven ministry. I pray God will show me how to fulfill the passion I have for a different kind of Christian ministry, one that makes a difference.

Many of us share this student's passion for "renewal- and action-driven ministry." We go to church every week, but we wonder if the church is really all it should or could be. In our success-oriented culture, this question is often framed: "Is our church growing?" And usually growth means three things: more members, bigger buildings, and higher budget.

Is this all there is to growing in a way that makes a difference? Shouldn't we ask not just whether our church is growing, but what we are growing into? What is the purpose of growth? In Matthew 6:33 Jesus directs us to seek God's kingdom above all things. We are to seek growth not for its own sake but for the sake of the kingdom of God.

For guidance on what this means we turn to Ephesians. Ephesians is a dense, dynamic book—a book in which God's people are drawn into a constant stream of purposeful activity. One of the key themes in Ephesians is *power*. Hear how this theme recurs in 1:17-23:

> I pray that the God of our Lord Jesus Christ, the Father of glory, may give you a spirit of wisdom and revelation as you come to know him, so that . . . you may know . . . what is the immeasurable greatness of his *power* for us who believe, according to the working of his great *power*. God put this *power* to work in Christ when he raised him from the dead and seated him at his right hand in the heavenly places, far above all rule and authority and *power* and dominion. . . . And he has put all things under his feet and has made him the head over all things for the church, which is his body, the fullness of him who fills all in all. (emphasis added)

The first three chapters culminate in one of my favorite passages in Scripture, the marvelous benediction in 3:20-21:

Now to him who by the *power* at work within us is able to accomplish abundantly far more than all we can ask or imagine, to him be glory in the church and in Christ Jesus to all generations, for ever and ever. Amen. (emphasis added)

Passages like these in Ephesians make it clear that kingdom-focused growth is not an uncertain variable, like crop yields or stock profits. It is an inexorable force of unimaginable impact. The same power that raised Christ's body from the dead is now at work in the body of Christ, the church. So if you have a nagging sense that the church isn't fulfilling its potential, if you come to believe that the status quo isn't acceptable, if you hunger for authentic transformation and long to see "the working of God's great power" unleashed on this community and throughout the world—it might be a sign that you are catching a glimmer of God's resurrection power.

Author Eric Swanson likes to say that transformation is more like the North Star, a direction to pursue, than the North Pole, a destination at which we can arrive. So in what direction is Christ's resurrection power driving the church? If kingdom growth is our North Star, what is our compass? Paul's letter to the Ephesians offers at least four growth goals toward which God is leading and empowering us:

1. Spiritual maturity: We are growing into a more intimate relationship with Christ and knowledge of God, which leads us to reflect Christ's love and grace to others (1:5, 17-18).

When Paul prays in Chapter 3 that God would "strengthen you with power," what is the desired outcome? It's not what most of us would dream of doing with unlimited power. The first reason we need God's power is so that "Christ may dwell in your hearts through faith" (3:16-17). The second outcome in Paul's prayer is "that you may have the power to comprehend . . . what is the breadth and length and height and depth, and to know the love of Christ that surpasses knowledge" (3:18-19). Only by God's power can we truly receive Christ and know God's love.

This "knowing" is not just information stored in our heads. Knowing God leads to changes in our being and doing, as we see in chapter 2. As we grow in the knowledge of God's love, and as we are shown the riches of God's grace (verse 7), we are prepared to do good works (verse 10). Knowing God enables us to become imitators of God by living a life of sacrificial love, as Paul directs at the beginning of chapter 5 (5:1-2).

Paul writes in Ephesians 4:11-13 that the purpose of spiritual gifts is "to equip the saints for the work of ministry, for building up the body of Christ, until all of us come to the unity of the faith and of the knowledge of the Son of God, to maturity." Note that the work of ministry comes first, before the building up. We don't have to attain spiritual maturity before we can serve; rather, taking steps of active faith is necessary to generate spiritual growth. We see this understanding of spiritual maturity in the word of the Lord that Jeremiah recorded regarding the godly king Josiah: "He judged the cause of the poor and needy; then it was well. Is not this to know me? says the LORD" (Jer. 22:16).

Steve Humphreys also learned what it means to know God. In an "Experiencing God" class at his church in Knoxville, Tennessee, he read Jesus' words: "Ye visited me not" (Matt. 25:43, KJV). Though Steve had never before been to a prison, he sensed God directing him to visit a particular inmate. He followed through and was profoundly changed by the encounter. Steve's next step was to offer the "Experiencing God" class to prisoners. When the class came to an end, an inmate who was about to be paroled pleaded with him: "Don't forget us. When we leave, we need you more than ever." The message sank in. Steve quit his job and began a post-prison support program, which eventually developed into FOCUS (Following Our Choices Unto Success) Prison Ministries. FOCUS offers a wide spectrum of spiritual outreach and social service ministries with prisoners, former offenders, and their families. Countless offenders and their families have discovered the "love of Christ that surpasses knowledge," as Paul prays in Ephesians 3:19, because Steve studied Jesus' words and decided to act on them.

> *Growth means that the grace of Christ dwelling in us, and the gift of intimately knowing God through Christ, is empowering the church to live more intentially as a reflection of God's love.*

2. Reconciling evangelism: We are growing toward greater completeness and unity as the family of Christ (Eph. 1:4-5; 2:19-22; 4:15-16).

When our family moved to Kansas, we "imported" two sons from Pennsylvania—one whom I was carrying in pregnancy, and the other whom we'd recently adopted. So the concept of being destined for adoption as God's children in 1:4-5 resonates with significance for me. We are not only redeemed sinners but chosen daughters and sons, to the praise of God's grace.

God has also chosen others who have yet to call on God as their heavenly Parent. We must extend the blessing of God's grace. We must tell others the good news that God chooses them for adoption. Evangelism does not mean inviting people merely to come to church but to live in a family, to become "members of the household of God," as Ephesians 2:19 puts it. We tend to think of growth as multiplying, but here it has more a sense of inclusion. God is filling out our family.

This kind of growth requires the power of God to destroy the "dividing wall" of hostility that keeps people separate from one another and from God (2:14). Kingdom work of reconciliation recognizes that everyone has an irreplaceable role in building up the church as a living expression of Christ in the world. We hear this in Ephesians 4:15-16: "We must grow up in every way . . . into Christ, from whom the whole body, joined and knitted together by every ligament with which it is equipped, as each part is working properly, promotes the body's *growth* in building itself up in love."

One urban Presbyterian congregation learned a unique lesson on what it means to be "built together spiritually" in love (2:21). They began with a Bible study for homeless individuals, which attracted several people with HIV/AIDS. Eventually these relationships led to a Bible study at an AIDS hospice, which drew a number of gay, lesbian, and bisexual people to begin attending the church. This is what happens when kingdom growth busts down the barricades between chosen members of God's family.

> *Growth means that more and more people (especially those formerly considered unworthy or excluded) are coming to experience fullness of life in Christ as part of a united church family.*

3. Transformational good works: The church is growing toward becoming the "fullness of him who fills all in all" (1:23) as God places "all things" in submission to Christ (1:22).

According to Ephesians 1:11 God's plan for creation ultimately "accomplishes all things according to his counsel and will. In this verse we hear an echo of the Lord's Prayer in Matthew 6:10: "Your kingdom come, your will be done, on earth as it is in heaven." The church serves as God's instrument in answering this prayer, for Ephesians 2:10 declares "we are what he has made us, created in Christ Jesus for good works, which God prepared beforehand to be our way of life." These good works are not just random acts of kindness, but reflect purposeful movement toward a world that conforms to God's will.

Ephesians 4:28 provides an example of this transformation: "Thieves must give up stealing; rather let them labor and work honestly with their own hands, so as to have something to share with the needy." The rest of the world calls it a success story when a former offender becomes self-sufficient. But God's plan is not complete until this transformed individual becomes so valuable to the community that others in need are blessed by his or her contribution.

By the power of Christ's Spirit we cultivate seeds of radical transformation in every area of life that violates God's good plan. One suburban Baptist church has demonstrated this in their history of responding to social concerns with sacrificial boldness. After the assassination of Martin Luther King Jr., members voted to approve a risky proposal: mortgage the church property and set up a fund to empower the African American community. In the 1980s, concern over U.S. policies toward Central America led the church to become an underground sanctuary for political refugees. Several church members were arrested for their involvement. Later, when a group of teenagers broke into the church and used the gas stove for heat, initial concerns about the security of the building gave way to a call to address the human need. The church joined the local Interfaith Hospitality Network, a coalition of congregations providing shelter to homeless families. As the church's membership statement affirms, "We covenant as individuals and as a congregation to work with others toward peace, justice, and the wholeness of God's creation."

Our expanding works of compassion and justice serve as signposts of God's expansive purpose: "To gather up all things in Christ" (1:10).

Growth means that we who are being transformed by Christ participate in the transformation of the world, so that every area of life increasingly reflects the lordship of Christ.

4. Lives of worship: We are growing in our fulfillment of the calling expressed in Ephesians 1:12 to "live for the praise of God's glory."

Our overarching purpose and ultimate destiny is to glorify God with our lives. How do we glorify God? Times of praise and worship, pouring out our hearts in song or testimony, are essential expressions of God's glory. But the dynamic, holistic model of Christian life described in Ephesians makes it clear that we also bring glory to God . . .

- in our lives of growing love for God and our neighbor;
- in our church fellowship as a growing, reconciling family of new life in Christ; and
- in our participation in seeing God's will be done on earth.

Conversely, God is not glorified . . .

- when growth in biblical knowledge and personal holiness does not lead to putting love in action;
- when growth in membership or budgets comes without expanding the family of those who are reconciled through Christ to God and reconciled in love to one another;
- when growth in service activity does not reflect Christ's Lordship or lead to greater righteousness and justice; and
- when growth in any area aims primarily to make the church look good, or has its source in our own power and goodness.

Growth means that the church is bringing ever-increasing glory to God as a demonstration of God's gracious, creative, redemptive, transformative power.

Based upon these four growth goals, are we growing? I suggest asking ourselves four questions to assess our growth from a biblical perspective:

1. Are we developing a deeper knowledge of God that leads us to be more Christ-like and loving in our character and actions?

2. Are we inviting more people to experience life in Christ and welcoming them into God's family, and in the process are we breaking down barriers to love and unity?

3. Is our work contributing to the transformation of more areas of life in our church and community in which God's will is done "on earth as it is in heaven"?

4. Do our lives and ministries increasingly bring praise to the Lord and reflect God's glory?

However we assess our current status, Ephesians 2:8-9 assures us that this kind of kingdom growth depends on God's power and goodness, not our own. This is why prayer is so central to the growth process (see 1:16-19; 3:16-21; 6:18-20). Growth starts with being rooted and grounded in Christ's love (3:16) and allowing God's love to flow through us to others (5:2).

So let us consider: Who needs to hear of God's grace and to see it demonstrated? Who is being left out of God's family? What barriers of hostility still divide people? How might lives be transformed by God's love, through evangelism and discipleship along side services like economic development and mentoring? How can we use our gifts to provide for those in need? Where is injustice evident that can be brought into conformity with God's good will?

We do not set out to achieve benchmarks of size or activity. We take the next step of building on Christ, the cornerstone (2:20), toward God's redemptive intentions for ourselves, our church, and our community and world. Then God will be glorified in the church, as the Spirit does more through us than we can even imagine (3:20-21)!

Heidi Rolland Unruh is an author (*Churches That Make a Difference* and *Saving Souls, Serving Society*), editor (*Hope for Children in Poverty* with Ron Sider), speaker and consultant, equipping churches and nonprofits for holistic ministry. She also serves as policy analyst with Evangelicals for Social Action. Heidi lives in Hutchinson, Kansas, with her husband, Jim, who is pastor of Faith Mennonite Church, and their three children.

CHAPTER 7

PREACHING FOR
Justice and
Reconciliation

"I beg you—look for the words *social justice* or *economic justice*
on your church website. If you find it, run as fast as you can. Social
justice and economic justice: They are code words. Now, am I advis-
ing people to leave their church? Yes! . . . If you have a priest that is
pushing social justice, go find another parish."[1]

Predictably these words, coming from the mouth of former *Fox
News* talk-show host Glenn Beck a few years ago, did not sit too well
among justice-minded Christians. While some chose not to give such
inane remarks the time of day, others fired back. A day after Beck's
words aired, progressive evangelical activist Jim Wallis, for example,
publicly called for Christians to leave Glenn Beck.[2] And so went a
brief but intense exchange in 2010 between people who had very different ideas of the meaning of *justice*.

One positive result from the debacle was that it caused many
churches to clarify what they meant when they used the term *justice*.
What does it mean to be a "social-justice Christian" or a "social-
justice church"? Wallis's rebuttal to Beck included a reminder that
there are more than two thousand references to justice, righteousness, the poor, the orphan, the widow, the alien, etc., in the Bible.[3] So
it stands to reason that justice would occupy an important place in
the church's identity and activity in the world.

When we talk about biblical justice, we must also consider the ministry of reconciliation, for God ultimately desires the miraculous embrace between oppressed and oppressor. As maddening as the scope of God's love may be at times—calling us to love even our enemies—the picture of biblical justice is simply incomplete without the color of reconciliation. The Bible calls God's people to reflect God's desire for justice with reconciliation. In this light, missional preachers need to hone their sermon craft in such a way that their congregations become justice-and-reconciliation churches.

What is Biblical Justice and Reconciliation?

The word *justice* defies easy definition. Delineating *biblical justice* from its more abstract, philosophical versions narrows it some, but the concept is still gigantic. Nevertheless, we must try to arrive at a basic definition. As we consider the meaning of biblical justice, the following core elements emerge.

God's Nature

Biblical justice, first of all, assumes its source—God. The pages of Scripture ground the very idea of justice in God's nature.[4] Three dimensions of God's nature in particular give shape to biblical justice: God's righteousness, fairness, and love.

All that we understand to be right and wrong stems from God's righteousness. Justice refers to upholding what is right and correcting what is wrong. To do justice, writes Mae Cannon, "is the expression of God's righteousness through right actions."[5] It is to do rightly in our relationships with all people, for all are made in the image of God. As divine image-bearers, we know innately the difference between right and wrong, though sustained sin can certainly sear one's conscience. The biblical principle known by most as the "Golden Rule" is clear enough, however, for even the most damaged of consciences: "In everything do to others as you would have them do to you" (Matt. 7:12). Living this principle out—from our personal interactions to our participation in the public square of ideas and politics—is to do justice.

God's nature also reflects fairness, which is a close relative of righteousness. The demand for the equitable distribution of blessings and opportunity for all expresses gospel righteousness. To be righteous is to care enough for others that they too share in the bounty of God. To do justice is to strive for this kind of fairness. As Sarah Dylan Breuer quips, "When human systems distribute God-given resources in a way that places a small fraction of humanity in luxury while a billion people live—or die—on less than a dollar a day, can that be anything other than sin?"[6] It stands to reason that God, who is righteous, is angered by the misuse of power and position that unequally distributes resources to the point where human beings made in the image of God suffer and die.

And God is love. "Justice is what love looks like in public," says Cornel West.[7] Biblical justice expresses God's saving, liberating love, which the redeemed in Christ have experienced. That is to say, loving our neighbors is the greatest expression of God's love for us and our love for God. Julie Clawson connects the Bible's two-pronged law of love with justice when she writes, "When we choose to love God and love others, we have no choice but to treat others with respect and fairness . . . . If we are to truly live out the command to love then we have to act justly."[8]

A Necessary Bias

The nature of God as righteous, fair, and loving defines in large part the core meaning of biblical justice. But the constitutive core of biblical justice also includes a bias toward the poor, the oppressed, and the marginalized. The biblical story reveals a God who pays special attention to the underdog, precisely because of God's impartiality. Social ethicist Stephen Charles Mott explains: "Justice must be partial in order to be impartial. Only by giving special attention to the poor . . . can one be said to be following the principle of equal consideration of human interest."[9] I see this principle most clearly in the parable of the lost sheep wherein the shepherd left the ninety-nine for a moment to seek the one that had lost its way (Luke 15:3-7). Did the shepherd love the lost one more than the ninety-nine that were safe? Or did he pay special attention to it precisely because he loved all one hundred equally—and that one had fallen on hard times? God's impartiality necessitates focused attention on the most vulnerable in society. This is biblical justice.

Now, if those ninety-nine were somehow responsible for the one sheep's lostness—I think of Joseph's brothers, for example, who sold their little brother off as a slave in Genesis 37—then biblical justice would cry out against them. "God is not evenhanded," South African Archbishop Desmond Tutu said in a *Time* interview. "God is biased, horribly in favor of the weak. The minute an injustice is perpetrated, God is going to be on the side of the one who is being clobbered."[10] By implication, biblical justice does not only mean God's special attention to the clobbered; it also means God's judgment upon those doing the clobbering. René Padilla pulls no punches when he writes: "Because God is a God of justice, *in any situation in which power is misused and the powerful take advantage of the weak, God takes the side of the weak*. In concrete terms, that means God is *for* the oppressed and *against* the oppressor, *for* the exploited and *against* the exploiter, *for* the victim and *against* the victimizer."[11] Biblical justice, then, involves solidarity with and advocacy for the oppressed poor, as well as prophetic action against abusers of power and position.

Addressing the Roots of Suffering

Another core element to biblical justice is its demand to know and rectify the source of human suffering. It asks the "why?" question regarding the miserable lot of billions of human beings around the planet; it challenges the structures and powers that cause the misery; and it takes part in building systems that foster equity of resources and opportunities in order to address the misery.

This is justice work, which differs in practice from compassion work. "Compassion means to suffer with or to walk alongside someone by empathizing with their needs and experience."[12] As such, it focuses primarily on the immediate needs of suffering people. "Compassion responds to the effects of [social] problems. Social justice seeks to address their systemic causes."[13] To do justice is to address the root problems that lead to poverty, oppression, and marginalization. It has to do with prophesying (in the Old Testament sense of speaking truth to power) against laws that oppress, repress, or keep people down. It has to do with supporting, lobbying for, and creating public policies that ensure fairness for all.

In practice, compassion and justice ministries are different, but they come from the same source—namely, the heart of God that aches in the face of human suffering. So to belittle compassion to emphasize justice, or vice versa, is ultimately misguided. Compassion and justice go together.

Where Enemies Meet: The Ministry of Reconciliation

Finally, we must consider the ministry of reconciliation as part of the core meaning of biblical justice, for God's picture of justice ultimately includes the embrace of enemies across sexual, racial, tribal, cultural, political, and socioeconomic divides. The theme of reconciliation deserves its own section, but for our purposes it will have to suffice to consider it within the framework of biblical justice.

The Bible calls us to the ministry of reconciliation (2 Cor. 5:18-20) as an outflow of our being reconciled to God. Vertical reconciliation with God leads to a commitment to horizontal reconciliation with one another. The ministry of (horizontal) reconciliation can be defined as "the hard work of overcoming distrust, misunderstanding, bitterness, and even hatred between peoples" in the power of the gospel.[14] Within the framework of biblical justice, this requires a two-pronged objective of genuine repentance on the part of the oppressor and genuine forgiveness on the part of the oppressed. The ministry of reconciliation deepens the meaning and practice of justice in that it envisions a world of redeemed relationships not only between God, humanity, and creation (the big picture), but also between oppressed and oppressor, abused and abuser, afflicted and afflicter.

Many have referred to this dimension of justice as restoration or restorative justice. But I agree with theologian John De Gruchy, who writes, "The phrase *restorative justice* does not carry the wealth or warmth of meaning embedded in the word *reconciliation*. What needs to be done . . . is to recover the full meaning and rich texture of reconciliation, and to demonstrate its inseparable connection with the restoration of justice."[15] There is so much more we could say about the ministry of reconciliation,[16] but for our purposes, the most important feature is its integral connection to justice. We cannot fully understand biblical justice without being committed to God's vision of the reconciliation of all things in Christ (Eph. 1:10; 2 Cor. 5:18).

In light of these core elements, biblical justice can be defined as a God-shaped demand of the gospel of Christ that addresses the root causes of social inequity, advocating for those who suffer, as well as challenging the principalities and powers that cause their suffering. This understanding of biblical justice necessarily strives toward the vision of God's grand agenda of reconciliation, which includes the liberation of the oppressed, the repentance of the oppressor, and the restoration of the relationship between them.

Characteristics of Justice-and-Reconciliation Churches

In order to make the leap from this somewhat academic definition of biblical justice to church ministry, we must identify the targets of injustice throughout time. Broadly speaking, the poor, people of color, and women have been on the short end of the stick of injustice through the centuries. Many scholars have identified these three groupings as those who have suffered the most. For example, Cannon writes that "much of the world's inequality has to do with poverty, race, and gender."[17] Social ethicist Miguel De La Torre uses stronger language. Making the point that these three areas of injustice are intertwined, he writes, "Race, class, and gender oppressions are the three prongs of Satan's pitchfork."[18] To be sure, there are other forms of oppression (such as religious persecution and homophobia, to name two), but racism, classism, and sexism make up the "big three of injustice." And missional churches possessed by God's vision of justice and reconciliation maintain an acute awareness of them.

Challenging Sexism and Affirming Gender Equality

Justice-and-reconciliation churches, first of all, challenge sexism and affirm gender equality. I deliberately begin with sexism, because man's reign over woman constitutes the most fundamental of oppressions, considering that more than half of the world's population is susceptible to it.

When Americans hear the word *sexism*, they tend to limit it to discrimination against women in the workplace. Certainly being excluded from leadership positions, being shown less respect, or receiving lower wages for the same work simply because one is a woman represent very real cases of sexism. But Cannon reminds us that a global perspective requires that we also consider "statistics of female genital mutilation, forced prostitution, the sex trade, rape abuse, and assault. . . ." She asserts, "Throughout history, women have been systematically oppressed around the world. . . . This is . . . a deep and painful reality that women are viewed as less than men."[19] Indeed, global sexism is a fundamental injustice that must be addressed if the rest of what we do in the service of justice will bear the mark of integrity.

Justice-and-reconciliation churches view women not only as equal in the sight of God but also as full partners in the practice of ministry. Justice-and-reconciliation churches ordain people for ministry on the basis of gifting, not gender. I realize that I may have just lost the "complementarians" who may be reading this, as the issue of women in ministry remains a highly charged one with complementarians on one side and "egalitarians" on the other.[20] This book cannot tackle the complexities of this debate without hopelessly digressing.

As the debate rages, however, justice-and-reconciliation churches affirm an egalitarian approach to women in ministry, for if they must err, they have chosen to err on the side of equality. No church in practice is neutral on this issue; the question is where it chooses to stand while the debate goes on and on. In light of the evil of global sexism, justice-and-reconciliation churches affirm the worth of women not only in value but also in the practice of ministry. We do so in order to model something different, something just to the world, by the power of the gospel. From this position, justice-and-reconciliation churches are poised to challenge global sexism, defending the dignity of women and challenging evil social practices that oppress them.

Challenging Racism and Affirming Cultural Diversity

Racism represents another great injustice that millions of people around the world have suffered, and justice-and-reconciliation churches challenge it wherever they see it.

Racism is more than personal prejudice; it is prejudice that is backed by social and political power, which is leveraged in favor of one people over others. For example, in the United States where white dominance has been established, people of color may harbor bitter prejudice against people of Euro-American descent; however, by definition this prejudice is not racism because it lacks the political power to disadvantage them. In this sense, racial prejudice, which anyone can harbor in their hearts (and which incidentally also needs to be challenged on a personal level), is different from racism. Joseph Barndt, anti-racism trainer and organizer in Chicago for the last thirty years, defines racism as the lethal combination of "race prejudice and the misuse of power by systems and institutions."[21] The unspeakable crimes against people of color through the centuries, from colonialism to apartheid to slavery to deprivation of rights and privileges, are acknowledged, confessed, and righted in justice-and-reconciliation churches.

On the positive side, these churches also affirm cultural diversity, as they are enraptured by the vision of the multicolored kingdom. In this racially intensified time in the history of our nation and world, the church has an unprecedented opportunity to bear witness to the wall-smashing power of the gospel. "For [Jesus] is our peace;" the apostle Paul reasoned, "in his flesh he has made both groups [Jews and Gentiles] into one and has broken down the dividing wall, that is, the hostility between us" (Eph. 2:14).

Justice-and-reconciliation churches take advantage of what celebrated missiologist Andrew Walls calls, "the Ephesian moment," a time when cultures have come together more rapidly and thoroughly than ever before to constitute the people of God.[22] As such, these congregations become attractive to the world. As Brenda Salter McNeil asserts, "When people see us living out the reality of being one, multiethnic, multilingual, multicultural and multinational family in Christ, it grabs their attention, piques their curiosity and causes them to wonder what makes us this way."[23]

The inauguration of Barack Obama as the forty-fourth president of the United States in 2008 was a monumental step forward for the United States—and in many ways, the world—in dealing with the evil of racism. However, to think the problem no longer exists would be incredibly naïve. When asked about the impact of Obama's presidency upon racism, former New Jersey Secretary of State and now pastor of a large African American church DeForest "Buster" Soaries forecasted that it will actually intensify, that it will get worse before it gets better, because the issues will surface and people will have to deal.[24] Justice-and-reconciliation churches have committed "to deal," by bearing witness to the multicultural gospel both by renouncing racism wherever we see it and modeling racial righteousness and reconciliation in Christ.

Challenging Classism and Affirming Economic Koinonia

The third prong of "Satan's pitchfork" has pierced the poor, those on the lower end of the socioeconomic class strata, throughout the centuries and around the world. Joining sexism and racism, classism keeps billions of people on the vicious cycle of poverty, which includes not just a lack of material assets, but also physical weakness, powerlessness, isolation, vulnerability, and spiritual and relational brokenness.[25]

Classism, which refers to socioeconomic prejudice with power, is insidious in that it ensures that the poor are kept *poor*. De La

Torre writes, "Missing from the discourse [of classism] is how poverty is caused—specifically, how through classism a certain segment of the population must be kept poor so that the dominant culture can benefit and maintain its level of luxury."[26] Whether they are the untouchables in India, gypsies in Eastern Europe, coal miner families in rural mountain areas of the United States, young women born into brothels in Thailand, or the homeless who occupy the streets of every city around the world, classism perpetuates the inequity that exists between the rich and the poor.

Justice-and-reconciliation churches challenge this evil, first of all, by showing no favoritism toward the powerful and wealthy. As a pastor, I know all too well the temptation to treat those with means in a special way, giving them prominence in the congregation. But justice-and-reconciliation churches do not succumb to such a temptation. In fact, they cultivate an atmosphere wherein the poor feel welcomed and lifted up in Christ. Furthermore, they form ministries that address the needs of the poor—feeding the homeless, establishing thrift shops, providing vocational training and financial management, and so on. Further still, they put their lives and reputations on the line in the service of the poor. I think, for example, of courageous churches of the past that participated in underground operations to free slaves, hid Jews from Nazi raids, and provided sanctuary for those escaping political or religious persecution.

These churches also encourage the well-resourced to exercise biblical stewardship and generosity, so that no basic needs in the churches will go unmet. I will say more about this in the next chapter. For now, suffice it to say that God calls the rich and the poor to be in "economic *koinonia*"—that is, "the sharing of material resources so none go without in the faith community," as part of the larger *koinonia* they share in Christ.[27] In justice-and-reconciliation churches, the rich and the poor worship together, pray together, minister to one another, and go hand-in-hand serving the world in mission for the sake of the gospel.

Preaching for Justice and Reconciliation

Preaching that is missional strives to shape God's people along the contours of justice and reconciliation, and I believe the following summary themes lend proper guidance toward this end.

A Just and Reconciling God

Above all, we preach that justice and reconciliation flow from the very essence of who God is and what God desires. God is righteous, fair, and loving. God pays special attention to the poor, oppressed, and marginalized. God goes to the root causes of suffering and makes things right. And God heals broken relationships, bringing oppressed and oppressor together for ultimate healing.

Jesus embodied kingdom justice and reconciliation. When John's disciples asked Jesus if he was the long-awaited Messiah, he replied, "Go and tell John what you have seen and heard: the blind receive their sight, the lame walk, the lepers are cleansed, the deaf hear, the dead are raised, the poor have good news brought to them" (Luke 7:22). And before his ascension, Jesus set in motion the reconciliation of the world in his name by sending his disciples to, "Go therefore and make disciples of all nations, baptizing them in the name of the Father and of the Son and of the Holy Spirit, and teaching them to obey everything that I have commanded you" (Matt. 28:19-20).

If we are faithful to preach the ultimate source of justice and reconciliation, then God's people will continue to live out this message, even if the current popularity of these themes fades away. God's people will continue to serve the poor, advocate for the oppressed, and strive toward genuine reconciliation between peoples, not because justice and reconciliation are chic, but because they are central to God's character.

The Gospel for Underdogs

Next, we preach for and on behalf of the underside of society. Proverbs 31:8-9 urges: "Speak out for those who cannot speak, for the rights of all the destitute. Speak out, judge righteously, defend the rights of the poor and needy." By doing so, we cultivate congregations that are welcoming to the poor, oppressed, and marginalized, setting a place at Christ's table for the most vulnerable among us. We preach the gospel for underdogs, for the kingdom of God is especially for them.

This type of preaching has at least two dimensions. First, it sharpens the eyes of the church to see those whom others do not see, to identify those on the margins, and to extend to them in word and deed the truly good news of the kingdom of God. Who are the marginalized in our communities? Single working mothers? Undocumented immigrants? The homeless? Ex-convicts? Gays and lesbians?

The elderly? The mentally or physically disabled? All of the above? Whoever they are, we preach in ways that reflect the theological truth that God is on their side!

After identifying who the underdogs in our communities are, our preaching also entails equipping God's people to a life committed to caring for, empowering, and advocating for them. It is not enough to identify who the underdogs are; we must also identify *with* the underdogs, being willing to sacrifice time, energy, resources, blood, and life for their sake as a testimony to the gospel. Preaching for justice and reconciliation is proclaiming the gospel for underdogs, equipping God's people to be committed to the radical purposes of the kingdom of God.

Prophetic Challenge

We also preach against the principalities and powers that perpetrate injustice, taking our cue from prophets like Jeremiah who cried: "Woe to him who builds his house by unrighteousness and his upper rooms by injustice; who makes his neighbors work for nothing, and does not give their wages" (22:13).

Or James, who did not mince words when he preached:

Come now, you rich people, weep and wail for the miseries that are coming to you. Your riches have rotted, and your clothes are moth-eaten. Your gold and silver have rusted, and their rust will be evidence against you, and it will eat your flesh like fire. You have laid up treasure for the last days. Listen! The wages of the laborers who mowed your fields, which you kept back by fraud, cry out, and the cries of the harvesters have reached the ears of the Lord of hosts. You have lived on the earth in luxury and in pleasure; you have fattened your hearts in a day of slaughter. You have condemned and murdered the righteous one, who does not resist you. (Jas. 5:1-6)

In the spirit of Jeremiah and James, our preaching must challenge social conventions that disadvantage certain people. It should rail against laws and policies that cause suffering among the masses. Anything less than that would be in danger of the "sin of omission"— silence in the face of blatant injustice. Historic examples of Christians who cried out against the powers perpetuating injustice would include Anne Hutchinson, who as early as the sixteenth century challenged male domination in society in general and in the church in particular;[28]

William Wilberforce and other abolitionists who fought against the seemingly immovable practice of slavery in the nineteenth century;[29] and Archbishop Oscar Romero, who paid the ultimate price in the twentieth century for challenging human rights abuses by the El Salvadoran government and its allies.[30]

Preaching against the powers cultivates disciples who believe taking on injustice is simply a part of living out the gospel. These disciples also know that taking such stands could be very costly, and our preaching should pull no punches about that. Our words need to instruct God's people to count the cost and be ready to carry the cross for the sake of the gospel.

Reconciling Love

Finally, we preach the reconciling love of God for all, even those who have committed acts of injustice. We learn from Jonah the subtle sin of self-righteousness, and we help our members see that God's love encompasses even the godless Ninevites. When we preach against sexism, we must be careful not to pit women against men, but to encourage women and men toward mutual submission and equal partnership for the sake of the gospel. When we preach against racism, we must not ultimately condemn the white race, but rather to lift up the vision of a beloved community of all tribes and nations, *including* the tribes that make up Europe and North America. And when we preach against classism, we must not ultimately condemn the wealthy, but rather see the poor and the rich in Christ enjoying the blessings of God and serving the world together for a more just and equitable world. If we do not preach in this way, then we may be inadvertently advocating for the oppressed, whom we are called to liberate, to become the new oppressors!

Does our preaching encourage God's people to love both the gay and the gay-basher, the Christian and the Muslim, those on the right and those on the left, the rich and the poor, and the shades of "red and yellow, black, brown, white" who are precious in God's sight? Does it create room for loving prisoners, drug addicts, and pornographers? God's love is all-encompassing and all-embracing, and we cannot preach anything less than that.

As we preach this gospel week in and week out, our churches become more poised to practice the kingdom in a world full of poor, oppressed, and marginalized peoples. In doing so, we become more

like the Master we serve, who came to "bring good news to the poor
. . . to proclaim release to the captives and recovery of sight to the
blind, to let the oppressed go free, to proclaim the year of the Lord's
favor" (Luke 4:18-19).

■ ■ ■

In "Who Me? A Call to Lead for Such a Time as This," preacher,
teacher, and author Brenda Salter McNeil inspires us to stand for
justice and reconciliation as she considers the story of Esther. She is
exhorting leadership, particularly to those who feel inadequate to
lead due to their social status. How does the sermon challenge injustice? How does it speak out for and empower an oppressed and
marginalized group?

NOTES

1. Glenn Beck on *Fox News' Glenn Beck* (March 2, 2010). http://media
   matters.org/mmtv/201003020048 (accessed August 10, 2010).
2. "Reverend Jim Wallis: Glenn Beck Is Wrong, Social Justice Is at the Heart
   of the Gospel," *Countdown with Keith Olbermann,* http://vodpod.com/
   watch/3226612-rev-jim-wallis-glenn-beck-is-wrong-social-justice-is-at-
   the-heart-of-gospel (accessed August 12, 2010).
3. "Reverend Jim Wallis: Glenn Beck is Wrong" (accessed August 12,
   2010).
4. C. Rene Padilla, "God's Call to Do Justice," in *The Justice Project,* eds.
   Brian McLaren, Elisa Padilla, and Ashley Bunting Seeber (Grand Rapids: Baker, 2009), 24.
5. Mae Elise Cannon, *Social Justice Handbook: Small Steps for a Better
   World* (Downers Grove: IVP, 2009), 20.
6. Sarah Dylan Breuer, "God's Justice: A Biblical View," in *The Justice
   Project,* 32.
7. Cornel West, quoted in Julie Clawson, *Everyday Justice: The Global
   Impact of Our Daily Choices* (Downers Grove: IVP, 2009), 21.
8. Clawson, *Everyday Justice,* 21.
9. Stephen Charles Mott, *Biblical Ethics and Social Change* (New York:
   Oxford University, 1982), 66. See also Mott's "The Partiality of Biblical
   Justice: A Response to Calvin Beisner," in *Christianity and Economics
   in the Post-Cold War Era,* eds. Herbert Schlossberg, Vinay Samuel, and
   Ronald J. Sider (Grand Rapids: Eerdmans, 1994), 81–99.
10. Desmond Tutu, quoted in Alex Perry, "The Laughing Bishop," *Time*
    (October 11, 2010), 42.
11. Padilla, "God's Call to Do Justice," 24.
12. Cannon, *Social Justice Handbook,* 32.

13. Cannon, *Social Justice Handbook,* 32.

14. Ronald J. Sider, John M. Perkins, Wayne L. Gordon, and F. Albert Tizon, *Linking Arms, Linking Lives: How Urban-Suburban Partnerships Can Transform Communities* (Grand Rapids: Baker, 2008), 66.

15. John W. De Gruchy, *Reconciliation: Restoring Justice* (Minneapolis: Fortress, 2002), 2.

16. For those who want to go deeper in the practical ministry of reconciliation, see Katongole and Rice's ten theses on "Recovering Reconciliation as the Mission of God," in *Reconciling All Things,* 147–151, and Robert J. Schreiter's *The Ministry of Reconciliation: Spirituality and Strategies* (Maryknoll, NY: Orbis, 1998). Schreiter also sums up Paul's teaching on reconciliation in the article "Reconciliation," in *Dictionary of Mission,* eds. Karl Muller, Theo Sundermeier, Stephen B. Bevans, and Richard H. Bliese (Maryknoll, NY: Orbis, 1998), 379–381.

17. Cannon, *Social Justice Handbook,* 119–120.

18. Miguel De La Torre, *Reading the Bible from the Margins* (Maryknoll, NY: Orbis, 2002), 54.

19. Cannon, *Social Justice Handbook,* 120.

20. For a concise overview of the complementarian vs. egalitarian debate, see Bruce Ware's article at www.cbmw.org/Resources/Articles/Summaries-of-the-Egalitarian-and-Complementarian-Positions (accessed October 17, 2010). Although Ware comes from a complementarian perspective, the article provides a succinct discussion of the issues behind the two positions. For a thorough explanation of the egalitarian perspective, Christians for Biblical Equality provides a concise statement in more than 25 languages. The English version may be found at www.cbeinternational.org/files/u1/smwbe/english.pdf.

21. Joseph Barndt, *Understanding and Dismantling Racism: The Twenty-First Century to White America* (Minneapolis: Fortress, 2007), 59.

22. Andrew Walls, *The Cross-Cultural Process in Christian History* (Maryknoll, NY: Orbis, 2001), 78–81.

23. Brenda Salter McNeil, *A Credible Witness* (Downers Grove: IVP, 2008), 16.

24. DeForest "Buster" Soaries in an advisory board meeting of Evangelicals for Social Action, Palmer Theological Seminary (October 8, 2008).

25. Bryant Myers, *Walking with the Poor: Principles and Practice of Transformational Development* (Maryknoll, NY: Orbis, 1999), 67–68.

26. De La Torre, *Reading the Bible from the Margins,* 74.

27. Sider et al., *Linking Arms, Linking Lives,* 48.

28. See Janice Bailey, *Those Meddling Women* (Valley Forge, PA: Judson, 1977), 13–25.

29. See Garth Lean, *God's Politician* (Colorado Springs: Helmers & Howard, 1987).

30. See Pilar Hogan Closkey and John P. Hogan, eds., *Romero's Legacy: The Call to Peace and Justice* (Lanham, MD: Sheed & Ward, 2007).

Who Me? A Call to Lead for Such a Time as This

■ ■ ■

Brenda Salter McNeil
ESTHER 4:12-14

Where do leaders come from? Are leaders born or made? It's quite common to hear someone described as "a born leader." This usually means that people have seen characteristics in that individual's life that suggest that he or she has the qualifications for leadership. But is it from birth that one is called to be a leader, or are leaders created by their context? Is it nature or nurture? Is it one's innate gifts and abilities or is it the context or environment in which one develops that produces a leader?

John Maxwell suggests that leaders are created by a combination of many factors. Some individuals may have particular gifts, skills, talents, and abilities, but there are also situations that cultivate leadership in unlikely people—people who don't see themselves as leaders, who don't prepare, and who don't believe they have the skills or the qualifications for leadership. But because of certain circumstances outside of their control, they have been thrust into leadership.

Such was the case with Dr. Martin Luther King Jr. He was not seeking to be the leader of the Southern Christian Leadership Conference, but the time demanded his leadership. I understand that when he and other emerging civil rights leaders were gathered in a room trying to respond to the challenges of their day, Martin's peers volunteered him to be their spokesperson, because he was educated, articulate, and understood the issues. But that was not what he wanted. My guess is that when they pushed him forward he thought to himself, "Who me? I don't want to lead this movement. This could cost my life. I want to be a preacher; I want to write books; and I want to pastor my church." But the time demanded his national and global leadership—and the rest is history.

So it was with the young Jewish woman named Hadassah whom we find in the book of Esther. She lived with her uncle Mordecai in a small village in one of the 127 provinces of King Xerxes. She was minding her own business, doing her own thing like any normal teenager. She likely had goals and aspirations for herself—things she hoped for. Maybe she dreamed of getting married someday, of having children and living a normal life, because life for her up to that point (in the words of Langston Hughes) "ain't been no crystal stair." Surely, there had been some difficult days in her short, young life. We're told that her mother and father are dead. What happened? How did they die? And why is her uncle raising her? Where were the women in her family? Wasn't there an auntie who could have taken in this little girl? We don't know. The text doesn't tell us. But we can surmise that there'd been hard-luck drama in this young girl's life. Nevertheless, her apparently single uncle educated her, trained her, cultured her, and nurtured her well. Things may not have been perfect in her life, but they were going relatively well now. She was in a home where she was loved.

Life was good, and Hadassah wasn't looking to lead *anything*. She was minding her own business, living her life. But unbeknownst to her, there was something happening in another province, far away from where she lived, that would demand her leadership. She wasn't aware of it, but the king in Susa was throwing a grand party. All of the *who's who* were there, and the celebration lasted for seven days. Food and drink and endless entertainment! At some point, the king must have run out of things to impress people with. In his drunken stupor (I surmise), he came up with the bad idea to show off his wife, Vashti. He sent an attendant to tell her to put on her crown and come parade for his friends.

The queen was appalled. No one was supposed to see the queen. In fact, people lowered their eyes and bowed out of respect for the queen. She was royalty and carried herself with dignity. When Vashti got word that the king wanted her to lower herself to the level of a common concubine, having men gawk at her, she could not believe her ears. So she sent word back to him and said, "I will not disgrace myself that way. I will not demean myself. I refuse to come. No." And she did not come.

This embarrassed the king, because Vashti's refusal was a blatant act of disrespect and a challenge to his authority. Everybody knew about it, and the men at the party told the king, "You can't allow this type of insubordination." They told him he should banish her from the kingdom. Because Xerxes was drunk—and surrounded by bad political advisors—he took their counsel. So the king banished his wife.

But after the party was over and the guests had departed, once everything was back to normal, the king was left there by his lonely old self. When he came to his senses, he realized that he didn't have a wife. Vashti was the only person who really loved him, who had enough respect not to give into his whims and wants, who had enough dignity and self-esteem to really be a queen—and he had banished her. Depression set in, so much so that those close to him said, "We've got to do something to get the king back on the throne. We've got to cheer him up." So his political advisors suggested that he have a beauty contest throughout the entire kingdom. The king once again followed their advice and ordered his officers to round up all the beautiful young women in the provinces and to bring them back to the palace so he could pick the one who pleased him the most.

So one day, when Hadassah was in her village minding her own business, unaware of the political decisions that would impact her life, the king's officers came and seized every young, beautiful, and eligible woman, including Hadassah. In a last-ditch, desperate effort to protect his niece-daughter, Mordecai told Hadassah, "Don't tell anybody you're Jewish. Don't reveal your ethnic identity. Don't speak in your native language. Don't let them know who you really are. Act like you're one of them. Use a Persian name. Call yourself Esther, not Hadassah." He said to her, "Behave like they do. Assimilate."

Why did Mordecai tell her to hide her ethnicity? Perhaps he knew she was living in a time like our own when people are too often judged by the color of their skin and not by the content of their character. Perhaps he knew that although she was pretty and smart enough to win, she would be judged unfairly and her chances to succeed would be limited if people knew who she really was. Like so many parents, Mordecai was trying to protect the girl he'd raised, so he told her to do her best to fit in, because in a world of racial and ethnic hatred, a person's life opportunities are diminished when those in power discriminate. That's what the evil of racism is all about. Mordecai knew racism and ethnocentrism were alive and well and would adversely affect his daughter's chances to succeed, so he told her to assimilate.

She obeyed—and it worked. Esther won the beauty contest! Her beauty, her poise, her gracefulness, and her intelligence worked in her favor, and she became the new queen.

At first, things went well for Esther in the palace. It wasn't what she'd planned, but life was good. Attendants waited on her hand

and foot. She had privilege, power, and position. Everything was going well until one day when she looked outside the palace window and saw her uncle Mordecai in sackcloth and ashes. He was a mess, weeping and wailing outside the palace gates. She sent her attendant out there with clothes to cover him up, but he sent the clothes right back. In essence he said, "I refuse to be placated or pacified. I refuse to be soothed. I will not allow you to shut me up or cause me to be quiet, because some things are worth crying about."

Brothers and sisters, some things ought to upset us. Some things ought to make us weep. When we hear about children being abused, lives being destroyed, or people being slaughtered in the streets, it ought to make us weep. We are not supposed to be indifferent to human suffering. Mordecai said, "I will not keep quiet; I will not shut up; I will not allow you to pacify me so that you can feel better. Some things are worth crying about!"

So Mordecai told Esther what was happening. He explained that there was a man named Haman—a very high official in the king's court—who was obsessed with people showing him respect by bowing down to him whenever he entered a room. Most people gave him exactly what he wanted. But Mordecai refused to bow down. The same man who had told Esther to assimilate refused to compromise his convictions. He believed only God was to be worshipped—that you couldn't give to any person what rightfully belongs to God—so he refused to bow.

That infuriated Haman. But instead of settling the score with Mordecai alone, Haman decided to kill all the Jews—Mordecai and his people. Why? Because of racism. When race and ethnicity come into the picture, stereotypes and generalizations cause people who look alike to be all lumped into one category. It is no longer just one person; it's the whole group. That's why if one black man commits a crime, all black men are considered suspects. If you get carjacked by one person, everybody of that color is a potential thief.

I can remember a time when I was guilty of this same kind of "stinkin' thinkin'." I was at the Laundromat washing clothes when two young boys came in to buy a soda from the vending machine. Their money got stuck and they didn't get a soda, so they began to bang on the machine trying to get their money or the soda to come out. It didn't work so finally they went to the manager—a young, Korean woman whose family owned the Laundromat. She tried the machine and nothing came out. Then she turned to those two young boys and began yelling, "Why you lie! Why you lie!" It was so harsh that I remember thinking to myself, "Korean people are rude." And then I had to repent immediately because I know better. I have dear friends who are Korean; they are my daughter's godparents, and they are not harsh or rude. In fact, they are some of the kindest, most loving, most godly people I've ever met. I was guilty of stereotyping, and that's exactly what Haman did.

Haman convinced the king he should get rid of all Jews. He said, "All the Jews are insubordinate. You shouldn't have any of them in your kingdom. They don't follow your rules, and they don't follow your customs. You ought to do away with them all. Don't tolerate them. And if you would let me get rid of them, I will make it profitable for you. I'll put a large sum of money into your treasury—375 tons of silver to be exact!" Let me hasten to say that whenever people are being killed and lives are being destroyed, there's almost always someone, somewhere, who is profiting from it. Usually it's someone wearing a crisp white shirt in a high-rise building somewhere far from the scene of the crime, someone with deep political connections, who is behind the scenes masterminding and benefiting from destroying people's lives.

Mordecai had to make Esther aware of Haman's plan. He told her, "You don't understand what's going on out here. You've become isolated and insulated in the palace. As a result you have become ignorant to what's really going on. You don't know what's happening to your people anymore." He made her aware that there was a diabolical scheme being devised to kill, annihilate, and destroy her people. "I know I told you to assimilate," he acknowledged. "I told you to watch out for Number One—to protect yourself. But the time has come for you to identify with your people. We need you to use your privilege, your power, and your position to advocate for your people. It's time! We need you to lead."

Esther's response was in essence, "Who me? You want me to go talk to the king? I could get in trouble. Don't you understand what you're asking? This could cost my life! You know I can't just go in and see the king. It's against the law. I would be breaking the rules. I could lose my position. I could lose my life. Who me? You can't mean me."

In a way, I can relate to Esther. In 1999 I sensed God calling me to a ministry of racial and ethnic reconciliation, but I had other plans for my life. "Who me? I can't do that," I argued with God. "Most of the churches that invite me to preach don't care about racial reconciliation. Most of the people who support my work and follow this ministry aren't interested in that. People might stop inviting me to preach. I might be marginalized and pigeonholed as someone who can only preach on one topic. People get killed when they start standing up for peace, reconciliation, and justice!"

But Mordecai said to Esther, and the Spirit says to you and me, "If you keep silent at such a time as this, relief and deliverance will arise from another place." Now that's not what I expect Mordecai to say. He was supposed to say something like, "Esther we need you! If you don't do it, who will? We don't have anybody else." But instead he said, "If you keep silent at such a time as this, then deliverance will arise from another place."

Translation: "If you won't do it, God will use somebody else." So the only question is whether or not you and I will participate in God's call, whether or not we will step into our destiny by getting involved in what God is doing in the world. Who knows? Perhaps you and I have been called to the kingdom for such a time as this.

For such a time as what? A time when people are being killed and lives are being destroyed; a time when people are being wiped out by ethnic cleansing; a time when there are wars and rumors of wars; a time when racial profiling is a regular occurrence; a time when people of Middle Eastern descent are being discriminated against, hated, and feared; a time when people are being annihilated by AIDS and pharmaceutical companies stand back and let them die because providing the necessary medicines is not profitable for them. Perhaps we have been called to the kingdom for such a time as this!

Then Esther understood what this was *really* about. This was about her destiny. Perhaps this was her defining moment. So she said, "Go gather all the Jews together and fast and pray for me. Do not eat or drink for three days. My maids and I will do the same. When this is done, I will go to the king, even though it is against the law. And if I perish, I perish." In essence she said to Mordecai, "You are trying to suggest that if I don't do it, I might miss my time. I might miss the reason for which I was born. But I understand this situation differently now. It's not about whether or not I'll lose my life; it's about whether I'm going to find my life." So she decided to begin her leadership in prayer. She fasted and prayed, and she got a plan from God that saved her people. It became her finest hour.

"There comes a time in every person's life," wrote Sir Winston Churchill, "when they are given a unique opportunity to discover the purpose for which they were born. It is their moment of destiny. And if they seize it, it becomes their finest hour."

Brothers and sisters, God is doing something great in the earth, and the Lord is looking for leaders who will seize the day. God's kingdom is coming on earth, and it will unite people from every tribe and every nation, and God wants us to get involved with what is happening. As followers of our suffering Savior, we Christians are uniquely qualified to speak a word of reconciliation, a word of healing, a word of justice, and a word of grace to a world that is desperately in need of the Prince of Peace. God is calling each of us to that task.

Your response to that might be "Who me?" And God says, "Yes, you—unlikely you, unprepared you, inexperienced you, uneducated you, teenage you, female you, senior citizen you, housewife you, college student you, recovering addict you, dysfunctional family you! For such a time as this."

Brenda Salter McNeil is president and founder of Salter McNeil & Associates, a ministry organization that exists to catalyze, convene, and coach Christian leaders in building multiracial, biblically inclusive communities around the world. A preacher, teacher, and leader in God's international movement for reconciliation, Brenda speaks around the world and has written several books, including *A Credible Witness: Reflections on Power, Evangelism and Race.*

CHAPTER 8

PREACHING FOR
Whole–Life Stewardship

More often than not, it's the little things we do in ministry that have the greatest impact. A member of a church I once served told me recently that my weekly prayer after offering helped him think differently about money, possessions, and his responsibility with what God has given him. He recalled part of my weekly post-offering prayer when I said something like, "Lord, help us remember that all that we have is yours, not just these tithes and offerings. We commit not just what has been collected in these plates, but also what we've collected in our bank accounts, our homes, and our properties to your purposes and to your glory. Amen." There was certainly nothing unique or earth-shattering about those words, but evidently they played a role in changing at least one member's understanding and practice of stewardship.

Stewardship and the American Dream

Stewardship: For the most part, in the words of Scott Rodin, "Pastors do not like to preach about it, nor do parishioners like to hear about it; few people write about it and even less read about it."[1] Why is stewardship so unpopular? I'm convinced that it has to do with the misconception that we, and we alone, get to decide how to manage our wealth and possessions. By the powerful vision of the "American

Dream"—the pursuit of the good life of upward mobility, comfort, security, and luxury—we have been trained to believe that we have the right to do whatever we want with our hard-earned wealth.

Authentic biblical stewardship not only challenges the individualism that fortifies the American Dream; it challenges the Dream itself. And by doing so, it threatens what we have been taught to be our basic inalienable right. It is difficult to be confronted with the possibility that our pursuit of the Dream has caused us to become greedy, materialistic, and consumerist; that perhaps we have taken the culture's cues and have chosen mammon over God (Matt. 6:24). Such thoughts—which get at the heart of biblical stewardship—prick, disturb, and anger good Christian people. So most ministers either steer clear of the subject or reduce its implications to the management of the church budget and its facilities.

Missional preachers, however, understand and teach biblical stewardship, encouraging God's people to use resources available to them for the advancement of the kingdom. And by doing so, we challenge the American Dream. In his courageous book, *Radical: Taking Back Your Faith from the American Dream*, megachurch pastor David Platt calls his congregation and all other U.S. churches to be part of what he calls "the Radical Experiment." In prophetic fashion, Platt challenges God's people with these words:

> I dare you to test the claims contained in the gospel, maybe in a way you have never done before. I invite you to see if radical obedience to the commands of Christ is more meaningful, more fulfilling, and more gratifying than the American Dream. And I guarantee that if you complete this experiment, you will possess an insatiable desire to spend the rest of your life in radical abandonment to Christ for his glory in all the world.[2]

Such preaching has taken The Church at Brook Hills in Birmingham, Alabama—Platt's congregation—in a wonderfully new and radical direction. From blindly embracing the church-growth theology of the megachurch (which can be viewed as "the American Church Dream"), to praying for the needs of the world and sacrificing what they have in the service of the spiritually and materially poor, the congregation at Brook Hills has begun to practice biblical stewardship.[3]

From Coins to Creation: Whole-Life Stewardship

Biblical stewardship is whole-life stewardship.[4] Far from reducing stewardship to keeping the church's annual budget in the black (by way of creative appeals for tithes) and occasional capital campaigns (such as special offerings for that much-needed educational wing), stewardship entails all that has been given to us, from the earth's abundant resources to spiritual and material blessings to our relationships to even life itself. "Nothing is left outside the realm of stewardship," claims pastor-teacher Bedru Hussein. "We are completely God's, including what we are and what we have."[5]

Hussein's words point to the essence of stewardship—namely, that nothing ultimately belongs to us; in fact, everything belongs to God, the Creator and Redeemer of all things. To be a steward, then, is to be entrusted by God to care for, manage, and cultivate that which belongs to God. This includes everything from our financial holdings to the environment and everything in between. From coins to creation, the call to be good stewards is an integral part of authentic Christian discipleship.

What would happen if Christians truly believed we've simply been entrusted with God's abundant wealth? What would happen if we truly believed our homes, our cars, our clothes, and our cash were, in fact, *not* ours, but God's? Internalizing this sense of God's ultimate ownership undergirds what it means to be a biblical steward.

A Careful View of Wealth

Certain traits accompany biblical stewards. First, we develop a careful view of wealth. By that, I mean we do not automatically equate prosperity with good. Contrary to the claims of the prosperity gospel (one of the most insidious "Christian" versions of the American Dream), wealth does not always indicate divine blessing. In fact, in light of Jesus' teaching that it is harder for a camel to go through the eye of a needle than for a rich person to enter the kingdom of God (Matt. 19:24; Mark 10:25; Luke 18:25), wealth might be a bad thing, a dangerous thing, a thing that impedes our salvation. Social ethicist Robert Franklin asserts, "The gospel of prosperity is a competitor to authentic Christianity."[6] Indeed, the insatiable pursuit of prosperity (which is nothing less than the love of money that Paul warns against in 1 Timothy 6:10) can place us at odds with the gospel. Accumulating material wealth as the pinnacle of success makes total sense in the secular utopia of the American Dream, but in light of biblical stewardship where riches might even be a liability, it makes no sense at all.

Furthermore, a careful view of wealth dispels the notion that the assets and possessions we do have can rightfully be used for our own personal ends (read: we can do anything we want with our money). As *entrusted* wealth, we should use our resources toward ends that are, at the very least, not contrary to the kingdom of God; at best, they should be used to advance the kingdom's agenda. As Tom Sine asks with prophetic hope, "Can you imagine the difference it might make if we in the Western church decided to steward all our resources in ways that intentionally seek to advance God's purposes first instead of prioritizing our own needs and wants?"[7] This attitude flies in the face of viewing our wealth first and foremost as the means for personal advancement, comfort, and recreation.

Kingdom Generosity

Such a careful view of wealth leads to a second trait of biblical stewards—namely, kingdom generosity. This is positively ironic: As we adopt a cautious posture toward the prosperity that may come our way, our eyes begin to open to the vast needs around the world—causing us to become lavishly generous. How can we become otherwise in light of the world's poor? According to *Global Issues's* "Poverty Facts and Stats":

- At least 80 percent of humanity lives on less than $10 a day.

- The poorest 40 percent of the world's population accounts for 5 percent of global income, while the richest 20 percent accounts for 75 percent.

- 22,000 children die each day due to poverty.

- Around 28 percent of all children in developing countries are estimated to be underweight or stunted. The two regions that account for the bulk of the deficit are South Asia and sub-Saharan Africa.

- An estimated 40 million people are living with HIV/AIDS, with 3 million deaths in 2004.

- Some 1.1 billion people in developing countries have inadequate access to water and 2.6 billion lack basic sanitation.[8]

And lest we think the United States does not have its own version of the poverty experience, Food for the Hungry Institute reports, "14.6 percent of American households (which consists of more than 49 million people) struggle to put enough food on the table."[9]

As followers of Jesus become more aware of these needs, the desire to alleviate the suffering grows. And as biblical stewardship takes root—as we begin to see God's resources primarily as a means to fulfill the agenda of the kingdom—we become a generous people, finding creative ways to give away our wealth (albeit wisely and carefully) such as "the graduated tithe" proposed by Ron Sider in his classic *Rich Christians in an Age of Hunger*[10] or the aforementioned "Radical Experiment" being conducted by the people of The Church at Brook Hills in Birmingham. The Advent Conspiracy, a movement that seeks to save Christmas from the spirit of greed, overconsumption, and over commercialization, is yet another model that has helped many Christian families and churches to truly celebrate Jesus during the holidays by genuinely reaching out to the poor and the lonely.[11]

In one form or another, authentic biblical stewards live out a kingdom generosity, giving abundantly toward the alleviation of the suffering of their hungry, thirsty, naked, and homeless neighbors around the world. After all, "How does God's love abide in anyone who has the world's goods and sees a brother or sister in need and yet refuses to help?" (1 John 3:17).

Commitment to Simple Living

Kingdom generosity is authenticated by a commitment to the simple life, a third trait of biblical stewards. Something is not quite right if we claim to be generous (or are viewed by the world as generous) and yet live luxuriously. Such generosity may be sincere, but does it not fall short of the biblical call to give sacrificially (Mark 12:41-44)? To maintain a truly generous lifestyle is to be guided by the question, "How much is enough?"[12]

Contrary to stereotypes, the call to simplicity does not come only from the radical, hippie, leftist fringe. For example, the Lausanne Covenant, a document that has served as the statement of faith and purpose for hundreds of evangelical churches and organizations around the world, states, "Those of us who live in affluent circumstances accept our duty to develop *a simple lifestyle* in order to contribute more generously to both relief and evangelism."[13] Biblical stewards know that the call to simplicity comes ultimately from Scripture. Biblical principles for the case include the equalization of wealth as seen in the Year of Jubilee when God commanded that all properties be restored to their original owners (stewards?) and all debts be cancelled (Lev. 25:8-38), the prophetic warnings against compassionless luxury (Amos 4:1-3; Jas. 5:1-8), and Jesus' establishing sacrificial concern for the poor as a prerequisite for discipleship (Luke 18:18-25).[14] Just like with kingdom generosity, the commitment to simplicity flows out of a biblically grounded and heart-wrenching awareness of the realities of poverty. As the Lausanne Covenant states as the basis of the call to a simple lifestyle, "All of us are shocked by the poverty of millions and disturbed by the injustices which cause it."[15]

A commitment to simplicity embodies a number of key missional values. First, it reflects God's concern for the poor. By identifying with the poor by living more simply, we bear witness to the God of the poor. Second, it puts us in position to actually address human need by way of freed-up resources and freed-up time. Third, it frees us to build community with one another. Rather than spending our time in the rat race trying to keep up with the Joneses, we avoid the rat race and have time to get to *know* the Joneses! And fourth, it challenges the idols of consumerism and materialism that so plague American society. Not that the United States is the only nation that bows to these idols; but in a land where there are more malls than high schools,[16] biblical stewards committed to the simple life bring gospel sanity to bear upon the out-of-control "lifestyles of the rich and famous" to which many people aspire.

The simple life looks different from person to person and from church to church, and we get into trouble when we sit in judgment against those who don't "do simplicity" like we do. Shane Claiborne of the Simple Way community in Philadelphia recalls a time when he flew to Toronto for a conference on simple living. Feeling pretty smug about how he and the rest of the folks at the Simple Way were exemplifying the simple life, Claiborne ran into friend and then-editor of *Geez* magazine Will Braun, who looked a little tired. When Claiborne inquired about it, he discovered that Braun, an advocate of the de-motorizing of society, had just arrived after bicycling a thousand miles to get to the conference![17]

For some, the commitment to simple living means having one family one car; for others like Braun it means championing the complete de-motorization of society. For some, simple living means organizing a neighborhood shed and sharing lawnmowers and tools; for others, it means living in intentional community.[18] For some, simple living means being mindful of their tendency to accumulate, and learning to buy less impulsively; for others, it means crusading against the proliferation of malls and the advertisement industry, which preys upon the weaknesses and cravings of the populace.

When our efforts to live simply become legalistic or judgmental, they violate what Richard Foster celebrates as "the freedom of simplicity."[19] However, while we must absolutely resist prescribing the simple life for others—thus perpetuating a new kind of legalism[20]—biblical stewards are compelled to ask themselves and the church the following guiding question: "If we really care about the poor, how shall we then live?"

Creation Care

Biblical stewards also demonstrate an acute appreciation for God's creation and therefore "walk gently on the earth."[21] The call to whole-life stewardship necessarily extends to earth-keeping; perhaps it should even begin there, for the earth is what sustains all of life and the rest of God's good gifts. Relationships, property, possessions, money—none of these mean anything if we have no earth on which to enjoy them! But more than a mere stage on which the human drama is played out, the earth itself is part of the drama. I see this in God's smile upon completing creation, thus validating creation as valuable in and of itself apart from humankind (Gen. 1:25).

The earth is also part of the drama in that God made humanity out of it (Gen. 2:7), thus establishing the organic interdependence between the earth and humans in their relationship with the Creator. Indeed, God, humanity, and the earth are in covenant community together.[22] Biblical stewards understand the integral connection between creation care and people care. "We are creatures of earth," explains sociologist Lisa Graham McMinn, "and so caring for earth is a way of caring for ourselves."[23]

Understanding the interdependence between the earth and people profoundly challenges the notion that earth-care has no place on the agenda of the church's mission. In the face of humanity's spiritual lostness and abject poverty, so the argument goes, how can we justify spending even a single penny or a single minute on caring for trees and animals and the like? Besides, didn't God sanction humanity to have dominion over the earth, to subdue it? Such thinking is rooted in our tendency to dichotomize and see things as radically separate; as if the way in which we care (or don't care) for the creation does not have implications for the way we practice (or don't practice) evangelism and work among the poor. The truth is, we serve a God bent on saving creation and everyone in it. Indeed, the reconciliation of all things includes healing relationships between people and God; between people and people; and between God, people, and creation (Rom. 8:18-25). Biblical stewards affirm this interdependence and understand that "the whole mission" must include the care of creation.

What does creation care look like? As with simple living, this is not a call for legalistic prescriptions and a judgmental spirit, but rather a call to keep ourselves accountable by asking tough, counter-cultural, anti-American Dream questions. On a personal level, do I recycle? Do I minimize the use of disposal goods? Do I turn lights and electrical appliances off when they are not in use? How would my house fare in an environmental audit? On a more corporate level, do we care about issues such as climate change, global warming, defor-estation, the mistreatment of animals, etc.? Do we support policies that promote the care of the environment? Do we practice socially responsible investing? As biblical stewards, we ask ourselves these kinds of questions and strive to "walk gently on the earth."

Preaching for Whole-Life Stewardship

The following four summary principles can help guide missional preachers in forming a church full of whole-life stewards.

The Good Life

First, we preach an alternative definition of the "good life," urging our members to pursue the Kingdom Dream over and against the American Dream. "The journey towards whole-life discipleship," writes Sine, "begins when we struggle to translate the vision of God's better future into a whole new understanding of what the good life is all about."[24] Sine challenges the stereotypical notion that to be Christian is to be out-of-touch with the real world and missing out on all the fun:

God does not call us to a life of self-imposed misery and asceticism, any more than He calls us to a life of more successful scrambling. We are called to a life that is much more festive, celebrative, and satisfying than anything the rat race can offer. God calls us to a good life that elevates relationships, celebration, worship, family, community, and service above the values of acquisition, individualism, and materialism.[25]

As I said earlier, authentic biblical stewardship is not a popular subject, precisely because it challenges what Sine calls the "the good life of the global mall."[26] It offends and angers people because the preacher is meddling into a domain that most of us Americans believe belongs solely to us. Furthermore, it can make us feel guilty for the lifestyles we live and the riches we enjoy; and heaven forbid if God's people start feeling guilty! As preachers, we must acknowledge that if we preach whole-life stewardship, members might leave and visitors might not return. As such, church-growth strategists would probably discourage us from preaching and teaching on it. It is true that missional preachers gripped by the vision of whole-life stewardship aren't likely to win too many popularity contests. But in light of the biblical truth of stewardship as set forth in this chapter, can we preach and teach anything less than the radical implications of the gospel upon our lives?

Relationships and Community: Investing in Human Resources

Second, we preach the priority of relationships, of community. Cultivating healthy relationships in family, church, and neighborhood is a stewardship issue in that we are investing in people, the greatest God-given resource. Many psychologists, sociologists, and theologians have documented the disastrous consequences of the quest for "the good life," which include dehumanization, alienation, and loneliness, even if one makes it to the top of the heap. But it doesn't take scholars to figure this out.

One of my favorite movies, often aired during the holidays, is *Family Man* starring Nicholas Cage and Tia Leone. In it, Jack Campbell (Cage) is a successful but desperately lonely businessman, who by angelic intervention is given a glimpse of the life he could have had if he had not chosen economic success over the love of his youth—Kate Reynolds (Leone). After just a brief glimpse of the love he would have experienced as a spouse, as a parent, and as part of a community of extended family and friends, Jack realizes the emptiness—the poverty—of what he had once thought to be the good life. Of course, if I had made the movie, I would have included the church! But the point of the movie remains clear: Relationships are more valuable than all the riches in the world.

What would happen if we measured wealth not by our investments in finances and property but by our investments in family, church, and neighborhood? We give mental assent to the notion that humans are the greatest of all the earth's resources, but I am not sure if we live as if we really believe it. But what if we did? Missional preachers keep this question before the people, and with it lead them toward a deeper experience of family, church, missional partnership, and human community.

Living with Global Poverty in View

Third, we preach a lifestyle that keeps global poverty in view. In chapter 3, I applauded the practice of Pastor Mark Labberton who, before Sunday service, would read the weekly update from a missionary family serving at-risk children in Cambodia. He did this so he would be "reminded of the realities of suffering in the world" and would lead Sunday morning worship accordingly.[27] Such a practice can only lead to "dangerous worship" that cultivates an awareness of unimaginable poverty experienced by billions of people around the planet.

We preach lifestyles that reflect this awareness—namely, lifestyles of kingdom generosity and commitment to the simple life. We preach sacrificial giving (where the tithe is only the beginning), such as what Platt urged his church as part of the Radical Experiment: "For one year," he pleaded, "sacrifice your money—every possible dollar—in order to spend your life radically on specific, urgent spiritual and physical need in the world."[28] We preach not just sacrifice, but the joy of sacrifice. It is better to give than to receive. From the perspective of the American Dream, this adage does not make much sense; but through the eyes of the Kingdom Dream, Jesus reminds us, "those who lose their life for my sake will find it" (Matt. 10:39).

We preach against materialism, consumerism, and the rat race, and we preach the rewards of the simple life. The rewards of freedom from the power of mammon, as well as the freedom to give more time to cultivate relationships and engage in God's mission. Missional preachers preach "the freedom of simplicity." Coupled with kingdom generosity, preaching the simple life equips God's people to take part in God's transforming work among the lost and the poor of the world.

Living with Creation in View

Finally, we preach a lifestyle that has God's creation in view. I once spoke at a student-led "green event" at the seminary where I teach. I walked up to the front carrying a baseball bat and greeted everyone while I pretended to smash a nearby table. Then I said, "This is the day that the Lord has made," while I pretended to smash a chair. And then I said, "I want to share the gospel with you," while I pretended to smash the windows behind me. If I were braver I would have actually smashed these objects to strengthen my point (but the seminary president was present and I valued my job!)—namely, that it is inconsistent to preach the gospel and destroy the surroundings at the same time. One cannot preach the transformation of the world and not care about creation.

We preach against a utilitarian view of creation that sees "God's good creation . . . as nothing more than provision of the resources needed to achieve [the American] Dream."[29] Over and against this understanding, we preach a biblical steward's view of creation, in which humanity is but a part—albeit a special part—of a greater ecological system created and set in motion by the God of the universe. We preach being responsible with all God has given us—including most fundamentally the earth that sustains us—and thus lead the redeemed in Christ into a harmonious relationship with God, one another, and the environment. Now more than ever, in this era of globalization, when the American Dream has become in a very real way the Global Dream,[30] the church needs to take up God's original call upon humanity to be whole-life stewards for the sake of the redemption of creation and everyone in it.

■ ■ ■

Social activist Shane Claiborne's "Radical Discipleship" offers an inspiring example of biblical stewardship as it challenges us to hold our possessions loosely and to invest in what is eternally valuable. How does the sermon call us to responsibility and generosity with regard to finances and material possessions?

NOTES

1. R. Scott Rodin, *Stewards in the Kingdom: A Theology of Life in All Its Fullness* (Downers Grove: IVP, 2000), 9.
2. David Platt, *Radical: Taking Back Your Faith from the American Dream* (Colorado Springs: Multnomah, 2010), 184.
3. To learn about the Radical Experiment, see "A Radical Proposal," www .brookhills.org/media/series/the-radical-experiment-2010/ and "The Radical Experiment 2010," www.brookhills.org/media/series/the-radical-experiment-2010/ (accessed November 23, 2010).
4. I first encountered the term *whole-life stewardship* in the works of Tom Sine, including *The New Conspirators: Creating the Future One Mustard Seed at a Time* (Downers Grove: IVP, 2008), 243–252 and the earlier *Why Settle for More and Miss the Best?* (Waco, TX: Word, 1987), 142–150.
5. Bedru Hussein and Lynn Miller, *Stewardship for All?* (Intercourse, PA: Good Books, 2006), 11.
6. Robert M. Franklin, *Crisis in the Village: Restoring Hope in African American Communities* (Minneapolis: Fortress, 2007), 118.
7. Tom Sine, *The New Conspirators*, 247.
8. "Poverty Facts and Stats," *Global Issues.* http://www.globalissues.org/article/26/poverty-facts-and-stats (accessed November 24, 2010).
9. "Hunger and Poverty Facts," *Bread for the World Institute*, www.bread .org/hunger/us/facts.html (accessed November 24, 2010). For a sympathetic description of a family of four living right at the poverty line, see Ronald J. Sider, *Just Generosity: A New Vision for Overcoming Poverty in America*, Second edition (Grand Rapids: Baker, 2007), 23–28. The statistics in Dr. Sider's book are a few years out of date, but the description of the difficulty to live below the poverty line is not.
10. Ronald J. Sider, *Rich Christians in an Age of Hunger*, Fifth edition (Nashville: W Publishing Group, 2005), 187–190.
11. For more about the Advent Conspiracy, visit www.adventconspiracy .org.
12. Platt, *Radical*, 107–140.
13. "Lausanne Covenant," in John Stott, ed. *Making Christ Known: Historic Mission Documents from the Lausanne Movement, 1974–1989* (Grand Rapids: Eerdmans, 1996), 33–34. Emphasis mine.
14. For a more just treatment of the biblical basis for simplicity, see Richard Foster, *Freedom of Simplicity* (San Francisco: Harper & Row, 1981), 15–51.
15. "Lausanne Covenant," 33.
16. Paul Lukas, "Our Malls, Ourselves," *CNN Money* money.cnn.com/magazines/fortune/fortune_archive/2004/10/18/8188067/index.htm (accessed November 26, 2010).
17. Shane Claiborne in conversation with Tony Campolo, "Lifestyle" in *Simply Enough* DVD (Alternatives for Simple Living, 2007).

18. See Sider, *Rich Christians,* 190–191. See also a short testimony of the Church of the Sojourners in San Francisco in Debbie Gish, "Creating a New Normal," *Conspire* 2/3 (Summer 2010), 48–49.
19. This is, of course, the title of Foster's classic book on the subject. See note 14 for full bibliographical information.
20. Foster, *Freedom of Simplicity,* 112.
21. This is the title of an excellent book on life choices that reflect genuine care for creation: Lisa Graham McMinn and Megan Anna Neff, *Walking Gently on the Earth* (Downers Grove, IL: IVP, 2010).
22. Zac Niringiye, "In the Garden of Eden I: Creation and Community," *Journal of Latin American Theology* 5/1 (2010), 18–31. In this insightful article, Niringiye makes a compelling case from the Bible's creation narratives for the harmony between God, creation, and humankind. All the articles in this particular issue actually affirm this harmony and call Christians to earth stewardship.
23. McMinn and Neff, *Walking Gently,* 24.
24. Sine, *Why Settle for More,* 112.
25. Sine, *Why Settle for More,* 144.
26. Sine, *New Conspirators,* 71ff.
27. Mark Labberton, *The Dangerous Act of Worship: Living God's Call to Justice* (Downers Grove: IVP, 2007), 33–34.
28. Platt, *Radical,* 196.
29. Sine, *New Conspirators,* 80.
30. F. Albert Tizon, "Revisiting the Mustard Seed: The Filipino Evangelical Church in the Age of Globalization," *Phronesis* 6/1 (1999), 3ff.

Radical Discipleship

■ ■ ■

Shane Claiborne
MARK 1:14-20

The African American evangelist-preacher E. V. Hill used to tell a story about a little old lady who sat at the front row of his church. When he'd get up and preach about all the things that were wrong in the world, this lady would say, "Get to the good news." He would preach about injustice and oppression, and she would murmur to herself, "Get to the good news, Pastor." He would talk about what happened on Good Friday on that old rugged cross, and she would say, "Get to the good news." But when he would get to talking about Sunday when Jesus rose from the dead, she would stand up and shout, "Now that's it! Preach that, Preacher!"

The good news is that we have a God who loves us even when we're full of wickedness. It's a message that says even a wicked people can repent. I think that all the bad news we hear all around us and read in the newspapers is a beautiful opportunity for the church to shine. This is what is happening in the first chapter of Mark's Gospel. The times were bad. John the Baptist had just been put in jail. But in verse 14 it says that after John was put in prison, Jesus preached the good news that "the kingdom of God is near" all over the town.

That seems a little odd to me. I wonder how I'd feel if I got locked up and all my community mates went out in the streets, singing, "This is the day that the Lord has made!" But, you see, Jesus knew the end of the story; it's almost as if Jesus is laughing at Herod, because he knows in the end that mercy will triumph, that God will triumph. It's no coincidence, I think, that the first folks to leave everything to follow Jesus were the marginalized: teenagers, prostitutes, fishermen. Rome's dream had failed them. They wanted something more to live for, or die for. The first folks to die for Jesus were people who had nothing else to lose except for the heavy yoke Rome had laid on their backs.

Indeed, the good news is good news to the poor. But it spreads beyond that, too; it can even reach kings and presidents. I remember reading something Gandhi wrote about his movement [of peace and simplicity] where he says, "We knew that something was happening when not only were the folks on the streets wearing homespun clothes that they had made with their own hands, but there were also members in parliament who were making their own clothes."

The movement of Jesus of building a new society in the shell of the old one was spreading all over the land because the good news is a call to liberation for both the oppressed and the oppressors. It's a call to leave everything and be set free from the meaningless toil and lifeless routines we fill our days with. God is saving us from ourselves. God is liberating us from our possessions that have come to possess us. And we find perfect joy, not by keeping all the stuff, but by giving it all away.

I met this one kid in India when I was there working with Mother Teresa and the sisters. We would throw these parties for the kids who were beggars on the street. One day it was the birthday of one of the kids I had grown really close to. It was about 100 degrees, so I'm thinking, "What should I get him for his birthday?" And I thought, "What better than an ice cream cone?"

So I got this kid an ice cream cone, and I took it to him. I had no idea if he'd ever had ice cream before, because he just stared at it and shook with excitement. And then his instinct was that, "This is too good to keep to myself." So he immediately yelled to the other kids, "We've got ice cream! Everybody gets a lick." He lined them up and went down the line saying, "Your turn. Your turn." Then he got full circle back to me and he says, "Shane, you get a lick too." I had this whole spit-phobia thing going on, so I kind of faked a lick and said, "Mmm, that's so good."

But that kid knew the secret. He knew the secret that the best thing to do with the best things in life is to give them away. That flies in the face of so much that we hear in our culture—and even in many churches with this self-centered, blessing-obsessed gospel of prosperity that's only about what we can get from God. And if we're not careful, we can lose the secret of God's liberation, which is: If you want to find your life you have to give it away.

There's a beautiful scene in that really weird movie *Harold and Maude*. This young man is proposing to this quirky woman named Maude. He gives her a ring as they're standing near the ocean, and he asks her to marry him. She says, "Oh, this is a precious gift." She looks at it and then she flings it into the sea. Harold says, "What did you do that for?" She said, "I love that ring. Now I'll always know where it is."

It's a strange way of looking at the possessions we have. And yet I think it's that sort of winsomeness that we have in Jesus, this holy recklessness with the stuff of earth that we just give it away because it is so good.

It's a lesson I've learned from our neighbors in North Philadelphia. I live in one of the nation's most economically devastated neighborhoods. We have 20,000 abandoned houses, and yet we have 3,000 families who are waiting for housing. We have 700 abandoned factories; it's just an industrial wasteland. About a year and a half ago, one of those abandoned factories caught on fire. The fire spread into our neighborhood and burnt down all our homes—the home where I was living, the community center, and about a dozen other houses. It displaced about 100 families.

I can remember, as it happened, there was this incredible thing called community that just burst out of the struggle. The Red Cross had set up a shelter nearby, but then the workers said, "The weirdest thing happened. Nobody stayed in the shelter because everyone in neighborhood opened their homes up."

I remember asking one of my neighbors, "How are you doing?" He said, "Pretty good actually. The greatest thing happened last night. For the first time I could see the moon because the factory had burnt down." I thought, "What a strange way of thinking of this." My friend actually made a mural of it. The mural shows this guy looking at his house as it's almost burnt to the ground. The moon is behind it and there's a little caption that says, "Boy, isn't the moon beautiful?"

I think it's that kind of freedom that teaches us to live as if none of this stuff around us even existed, to live as if the world around us is fading away and won't last. It's this call to know that there's something deeper at the core of everything. This is the call to liberation.

I find it funny when people hear that we've left a lot of this stuff to follow Jesus and they say, "Oh, it's so heroic that you take a vow of simplicity." And I say, "You must have never seen the pearl that we left everything for" (Matt. 13:45). We said no to some things, but we said yes to something so dazzling and beautiful that it makes all the other stuff look like dung.

We've said no to the counterfeit peace of Rome, but we've said yes to the perfect peace of Jesus. We've said no the myth of redemptive violence, but we've said yes to the truth of redemptive grace. We've said no to the illusion of independence, but we've said yes to the beautiful interdependence of the family of God. We've said no to the American Dream, but we've said yes to a dream that burns much brighter.

We've left everything for the pearl, but the things we've left are like fool's gold. It's like cubic zirconium. It's like that plastic jewelry, that counterfeit pearl, the gaudy stuff that just clutters our lives. It's not about what we've left; it's about what we've found. We've found a love that's worth saying yes to.

And that's why disciples left their nets; that's why they died. They died because this Jesus is so beautiful. And as liberated people, I think that frees us up to laugh a little bit. We can laugh at the jails, because we know we have a God who liberates the captives. We can laugh at the recession because we know our providence comes from somewhere else.

I love that story in Revelation 18 about the fall of Babylon. Revelation says there were two responses to the fall. There was the response of the merchants who looked up and wept and beat their chests and said, "Oh, how could great Babylon fall?" And then there was the response of the angels. It says the angels rejoiced and said, "Fallen, fallen, is the great whore, Babylon." And maybe the big question for us is: Are we weeping with the merchants or laughing with the angels today?

In my neighborhood, I've learned to laugh. I think poor folks get it because they can rejoice when the world around us seems to be falling apart. They're not too stunned when kings or presidents fail us because they've never had much faith in Caesars. The poor can laugh when Babylon falls because they know the New Jerusalem is coming. They can laugh when markets collapse because they know their providence comes from God. And like the lilies and the sparrows, they have the freedom because they've never really trusted in a 401(k)—or is it a 201(k) now? There's that freedom that says, "We're just praying for our daily bread."

One of my neighbors told me, "Oh, we're going to make it through. God is still good. And besides, my people have been in a recession for a few hundred years." It's with that freedom that we say, "Our hope today does not lie on Wall Street; our hope doesn't rest in America; our hope does not come from a new Caesar or even a new president. [As the hymn writer Edward Mote declared,] "Our hope is built on nothing less than Jesus' blood and righteousness. On Christ the solid rock we stand. All other ground is sinking sand."

Indeed, as we look around, we see that all other ground is sinking sand. But Christ will live forever. In the name of the Father, Son, and the Holy Spirit. Amen.

Shane Claiborne is one of the founding members of The Simple Way, a community in Philadelphia, Pennsylvania, that has helped to define the New Monastic Movement in the United States and beyond. Shane is a prominent activist, renowned speaker, and author of many books including *The Irresistible Revolution, Jesus for President,* and *Becoming the Answer to Our Prayers.*

CHAPTER 9

PREACHING FOR SHALOM:
Life and Peace

In college, I joined the right-to-life movement, having been profound-ly convinced that abortion-on-demand was the unjustifiable taking of human life. Years later, while serving as a pastor, I joined with many other clamoring voices and marching feet in protesting the pre-emptive war that the United States declared on Iraq in particular and on global terrorism in general. And now as I write, I am a part of an interfaith movement in my city that seeks to prevent gun vio-lence, which cuts short the lives of thousands of youth not only in the streets of inner cities but also in the school hallways of the suppos-edly safer suburbs. As I reflect upon the causes that have inspired me to action through the years, a common conviction has driven them—namely, the sacredness of life and the ethical call to resist the violence that seeks to destroy it.

To fight against violence and destruction—or more positively, to protect life and to work toward peace—seems agreeable enough to all. After all, "only psychopaths and sociopaths can without remorse destroy the lives of others,"[1] and "No sane human being would say that war and conflict are preferable to peace."[2] And yet, just from the short list of issues in which I have been involved as an activist through the years, I can verify that good Christian people find them-selves on the opposite sides of each of these issues. Most of my allies in the fight against abortion, for example, are conservative evangeli-cals, who view protesting U.S.-declared war as unpatriotic and who see efforts to prevent gun violence prevention as somehow trampling on the Second Amendment right to bear arms. And many of my allies in denouncing war and curbing gun violence are political and theological progressives who see a woman's right to choose as paramount over the life of her unborn child. In my own deepening understanding of the values of the kingdom of God, I cannot help but see the inconsistency within both conservative and progressive positions.

Shalom (Life and Peace) in a Violent World

I realize that issues such as abortion and war—the issues most people associate with life and peace respectively—are extremely sensitive; as such, to make a case for the relationship between life and peace can potentially offend just about everyone! But it is my hope that the life-peace connection can serve as a bridge across the conservative-progressive divide, for I am convinced that the gospel of life and the gospel of peace are the same gospel. We are called to be both "pro-life" and "pro-peace" in the most authentic sense of these terms. Unfortunately, these "pro-" terms are hopelessly loaded, as political ideologues and activists have co-opted them for their own ends. As such, they are limited in their ability to create a bridge between those who protect life and those who make peace.

Several Christian social activists-theologians in the 1980s and '90s, such as the late Cardinal Joseph Bernardin and Ronald J. Sider, did significant "bridge work" across party lines by employing terms such as *consistent life ethic*,[3] *completely pro-life*,[4] and *the seamless garment*,[5] thus creating language for people who desire to live and vote according to the higher laws of life and peace.

Whatever terminology we use for this bridge work, it refers to "a moral commitment to respecting, protecting, and enhancing human life at every stage and in every context."[6] The purpose statement of the organization appropriately called "Consistent Life: Voices for Peace and Life" provides a practical angle to the definition, by stating, "We serve the anti-violence community by connecting issues, building bridges, and strengthening the case against each kind of socially-approved killing by consistently opposing them all."[7]

As terms go, I like the word *shalom* to convey the consistency between life and peace, not only because of its conciseness, but more importantly because it captures the biblical vision of wholeness. Translated most often in the English as "peace," it can also be defined as "the fullness of life."[8] *Shalom* is what results when God reigns as

Redeemer and Lord. Life and peace characterize *shalom* existence. Other core elements, such as mercy, justice, and the restoration of creation are also part of *shalom*; and when I say *life* and *peace,* I surely keep these other things in mind. As the National Council of Catholic Bishops' "Challenge of Peace" statement says, "No society can live in peace with itself, or with the world, without a full awareness of the worth and dignity of every human person."[9]

The fundamental enemy of life and peace is death-dealing violence, which manifests on every level of human existence, from world wars to hatred in the human heart, and everything in between. According to the biblical story, humanity's propensity toward violence is a consequence of the Fall in Genesis 3; indeed, the first murder is recorded in the very next chapter when Cain killed Abel (Gen. 4:8-10). According to Walter Wink, "The Fall affirms the radicality of evil."[10] And this evil includes humanity's bent toward violence. Wink goes on to say that the Fall points to a deeper reality of the human condition—"a layer of sludge beneath the murky waters that can be characterized only as a hellish hatred of the light, of truth, of kindness and compassion, *a brute lust for annihilation.*"[11] From cyber-bullying to domestic abuse, from homicide to genocide, from terrorism to torture to drive-by shootings, we live in a dangerously violent world.[12] The gospel of the kingdom counteracts this violence by offering "the third way" of Jesus, which essentially refers to the way of nonviolent engagement.[13] I will say more about this shortly.

Cultivating *Shalom,* a Culture of Life and Peace

Peace activists Alan Kreider, Eleanor Kreider, and Paulus Widjaja make a biblical case for the church to become "a culture of peace . . . in which unreconciled enemies are reconciled . . . unforgiven people are forgiven and . . . they are given a common mission—to share the 'good news of peace' with all nations."[14] I am drawn to this description of the church as "a culture of peace." And given the connection between life and peace, it makes sense to extend it to "a culture of life and peace," i.e., a culture of *shalom.* What are some characteristics of Christians and churches that are being cultivated in the fertile soil of *shalom?*

Respect for Life at Every Stage

I have already laid the groundwork for this characteristic, but a brief expansion of it here locates it among the core elements of a *shalom* person and a *shalom* church. To ones who have been restored in Christ to a right relationship with God, the Creator and Giver of Life, life takes on intrinsic value. Lutheran bishop Lowell Erdahl points out, "While Christianity has no monopoly on reverence for life, it is a central Christian affirmation."[15] Biblical faith teaches that life has intrinsic value because God created it (Gen. 1–2). Furthermore, human life carries particular value because humans were created in God's own image (Gen. 1:26-27). Zac Niringiye notes, "Whereas the other creatures are made 'according to their kinds,' humanity is made 'in [God's] image, in [God's] likeness.'"[16] As such, although all life warrants our respect, human life deserves our deepest and highest respect.

As if it is not enough to value life simply because God created it, we should also consider the truth that "For God so loved the world that he gave his only Son, so that everyone who believes in him may not perish but may have eternal life" (John 3:16). "It is crucial to see," asserts Ron Sider, "that the biblical teaching about eternal life does not refer to some ethereal, spiritual fairyland totally unrelated to human history and the created order."[17] In other words, the idea of eternal life is not limited to a future bliss but also to abundant life now (John 10:10). Apparently, God deemed the world valuable enough to heal, and every human life as valuable enough to save in Jesus Christ. Furthermore, asserts Baptist ethicist David Gushee:

> Every life means every life, without exception. That includes two-month-along developing human beings in the womb, poor babies in Bangladesh, impoverished children in ghettos, abused wives and children, civilians in war zones, wounded soldiers at Walter Reed, imprisoned detainees in the war on terror, aging people in nursing homes, mentally handicapped people, people convicted of heinous crimes. Everyone.[18]

Based upon the life-giving doctrines of creation and redemption, a person's worth is not based upon his or her age, physical or mental condition, socioeconomic status, or usefulness in society. As Christians, we need no other reason to affirm the value of human life than the fact that each and every human being is made in the image of God and is profoundly loved by God. To do violence to the living therefore—to harm, injure, kill—is wrong. "Thou shall not kill" (Ex. 20:13).

One of the most powerful and beautiful truths about the death and resurrection of Christ is that the final enemy of death has been defeated (1 Cor. 15:54-57). Through Jesus' ministry of life-giving words, liberating deeds, atoning death, and resurrection power, life—and not death—has become the final word for all time. As a result in the power of the Spirit, followers of Jesus—*shalom* people— challenge death and all its ways, resisting unthinking absolutism and respecting life at every stage from womb to tomb.

We need to be prayerfully sensitive to extreme cases in which the tragic choice to end a life may be permissible, such as when one life is endangered by another. However, I believe societies go tragically awry when they make exceptions the law of the land, such as abortion-on-demand, capital punishment, and preemptive war.[19] I could say more here about these types of exceptions (and probably should); but rather than focus on them, I want to stress the normative rule for *shalom* people—namely, to respect, defend, and protect life, from the unborn to the elderly and all in between who are threatened by the death-dealing violence of this world.

Human Flourishing

But *shalom* is not satisfied with merely the defense and protection of life; it seeks the fullness of life. Another way of putting it is that *shalom* people are ultimately not "anti-" people but "pro-" people. We are truly "pro-life" in the sense that we participate in activities and institutions that cultivate *human flourishing*. Although human flourishing is a largely philosophical term that has synonyms such as *happiness, self-actualization, empowerment,* or *transformation,* I believe the term is especially effective in conveying the *shalom* image of human beings blossoming to their full potential in harmony with God, one another, and the rest of creation. An InterVarsity Christian Fellowship document introducing a conference on human flourishing states, "We are called to nurture life within ourselves, our communities, and in our world. Abundant life is a quality of the kingdom of God, and from this root grows our commitment to human flourishing."[20] Being truly *for* life and not just *against* death, *shalom* Christians seek to enable all persons, from conception to old age, to flourish in the name of Jesus Christ and by the power of the Spirit.

Practically, this commitment to human flourishing means helping broken, vulnerable people—those diminished by poverty, oppression, and conflict—move toward wholeness. In the words of theologian Vinay Samuel, "[The poor] need their personhood . . . restored."[21] Samuel goes on to elaborate on ten dimensions of personhood, which include the physical, psycho-emotional, social, ethical, and spiritual areas of the human person that need restoration and development.[22] For those who are against abortion, for example, a commitment to human flourishing should manifest in activities such as finding adoptive homes for children, taking in foster children, and supporting ministries to assist young, single mothers. And for those who protest gun violence and war, a commitment to human flourishing should be expressed in activities such as caring for veterans, grieving with families who have lost loved ones to war, and participating in reconciliation work between warring factions.

Our mission toward human flourishing—our proactive striving to help fellow human beings reach their God-envisioned potential (even as we strive to do this ourselves)—is the necessary affirmative aspect of our commitment to *shalom,* which "calls us to reverence life, to support everything that enhances and ennobles life and to oppose everything that degrades and destroys life."[23]

The Way of Nonviolence

The way of nonviolent engagement constitutes a third characteristic of *shalom* people. We take seriously the teachings of the Master to love our enemies (Matt. 5:43-48) and to put away the sword (Matt. 26:42), and we interpret Jesus' death on the cross as his way of overcoming hate with love and evil with good (Matt. 26:53; Rom. 12:17-21). We see neither retaliation nor passivity as acceptable responses to the world's death-dealing violence; we see a third way.

Popularized by New Testament scholar Walter Wink, this "third way" is the radical way of nonviolent resistance, based primarily upon the teachings of Jesus concerning turning the other check, giving one's undergarment, and going the second mile (Matt. 5:38-42; Luke 6:29-30). Contrary to popular interpretations that these illustrations teach victims to subject themselves to further humiliation and pain in response to bully tactics, Wink shows that they actually convey resistance by denying a bully the power to humiliate while simultaneously seizing the moral initiative in the situation. For example, in Jesus' time and culture, "turning the other cheek" would force an offender to strike the victim on the left cheek, which was willfully offered. But this action actually elevates the victim to equal social status—the exact opposite of what the striker intended. Non-violent resistance disarms the violator while maintaining the dignity of the victim. According to Wink, this and the other two illustrations demonstrated a third way of response to dominant violators of human dignity and life—not the first way of violent retaliation nor the second way of cowering acquiescence, but the third way of non-violent, righteous resistance.[24]

Wink cautions that we must be responsible in teaching nonviolence to victims of domestic abuse, racism, and the like, lest we teach them the way of passivity and cowardice.[25] I agree, but we still need more to concretize nonviolent righteous resistance in our lives. Peace activist Richard K. Taylor offers five principles that I believe can help guide *shalom* Christians in the way of gospel nonviolence:[26]

1. A deep faith in God and God's power (Rom. 1:16; 2 Thess. 1:11). Gospel nonviolence is so contrary to fallen human nature that it takes nothing less than deep faith to enable us to practice it—even for Jesus (see Matt. 26:39).

2. A resolve to resist injustice—or, stated more positively, a strong sense of justice (Jer. 7:5-7; Mic. 6:8).

3. Goodwill toward wrongdoers (Luke 6:35-36; Rom. 12:14-21).

4. A willingness to suffer for what is right (Matt. 5:10-12; 1 Pet. 2:19-21).

5. A refusal to inflict suffering on others (Zech. 7:9-10; Matt. 22:39).

If these guiding principles seem superhuman, it is because they are; go back to Principle 1!

Waging Peace

Finally, *shalom* Christians understand the proactive aspect of peace—namely, the call to make peace, to initiate it and help shape the world by it. It is not enough to keep the peace or to respond nonviolently to enemies of peace; we must also advance to make peace. Jesus said, "Blessed are the peace*makers,* for they will be called children of God" (Matt. 5:9). I confess that my heart warms when I pass a vehicle sporting the bumper sticker, "Wage Peace" (attesting to the fact that once in a great while, a bumper sticker gets it right!).

To wage peace takes on at least three practical dimensions. First, *shalom* Christians forgive, as they bask in God's forgiveness for them (Matt. 6:14-15). A church cannot promote peace in the world unless it learns to extend forgiveness even to those who have done great harm. The story of Eric Irivuzumugabe comes to mind. A Tutsi who survived the infamous Rwandan genocide, Irivuzumugabe learned to forgive Hutus, who massacred many of his loved ones and friends.[27] The story of the Amish community that extended forgiveness to the man who murdered five of their children and injured five others in a school shooting in Nickel Mines, Pennsylvania, also comes to mind.[28] These stories speak of "the divine logic of forgiveness."[29] To forgive is to wage peace.

Second, inseparably related to forgiveness is the practice of reconciliation. We are commanded not just to love our neighbors but also to love our enemies. The ministry of reconciliation ensures that forgiveness goes the distance (Rom. 5:18-20). In a sermon on loving our enemies, Dr. Martin Luther King Jr. preached, "We can never say, 'I will forgive you, but I won't have anything further to do with you.' Forgiveness means reconciliation, a coming together again. Without this, no man can love his enemies."[30]

And third, *shalom* Christians engage in subversive acts of compassion and justice. By "subversive" I mean to emphasize that we aid those suffering due to political conflict or injustice, not just because they need desperate help, but also as a statement to the powers that their decisions destroy lives. To wage peace is to oppose war and injustice by helping the suffering poor who are so often caught in the crossfire.

Preaching for *Shalom*

The following three guidelines can help us as missional preachers who aim to cultivate *shalom* in our congregations.

Consistent Ethic of Life and Peace

We preach a commitment to life because we are committed to peace, and we preach a commitment to peace because we are committed to life. We see the relational consistency between them in the kingdom of God, so we preach life and peace together. "To set the mind on the flesh is death," penned the apostle Paul, "but to set the mind on the Spirit is life and peace" (Rom. 8:6). We preach this consistent ethic despite pressure to conform to a particular political ideology.

As both conservatives and liberals draw their lines in the sand, it becomes increasingly more difficult for people to challenge any part of the respective agendas of the right or the left. "The power of Party identity is so profound," writes Gushee, "that otherwise thoughtful people lose the capacity for independent reflection."[31]

God forbid that conservatives question American-declared war or help in the work of gun violence prevention, and God forbid that progressives join in the fight against abortion-on-demand or speak out against the dehumanization of women through pornography. Gushee speaks for himself, but captures the conviction needed for missional preaching, when he declares, "As a Christian, I believe that no force is to be allowed to compete with God's word for the government of my life in any aspect. This includes Party loyalty."[32] Preaching for *shalom* does not cater to left or right ideologies; we preach the kingdom God, which respects and promotes life from womb to tomb, consistently and courageously.

Forgiveness and Reconciliation

We preach forgiveness and reconciliation, which are fundamental to the good news of Christ. They are fundamental in the sense that the Christian faith rests completely on the God who has seen fit to forgive and reconcile. In response, we extend forgiveness and reconciliation to others. The parable of the wicked slave in Matthew 18 forcefully illustrates this. We know the story: In his mercy, the king forgave a slave of all his debt. But later on that same slave found another slave who owed him money, and when the second slave could not pay, the first slave had him thrown in jail. When the king found out, he told the one he had forgiven, "You wicked slave! I forgave you all that debt because you pleaded with me. Should you not have had mercy on your fellow slave, as I had mercy on you?" The king then had him imprisoned until he paid his whole debt (Matt. 18:21-35).

Kreider and colleagues note, "God's command to his people is not simply to accept his forgiveness; it is to act forgivingly to other people. It is not simply to be reconciled to God; it is to be reconciled to other people."[33] Preaching for *shalom* calls God's people to forgive others as our heavenly Father has forgiven us (Matt. 6:14-15; 18:21-35), and it calls us to seek reconciliation wherever conflict and brokenness reside, just as God has reached out to be reconciled to us (2 Cor. 5:18-20).

Peacemaking unto Death

And we preach sacrificial peacemaking. We preach that "a harvest of righteousness is sown in peace for those who make peace" (Jas. 3:18). As the late Vernon C. Grounds once preached, "The God of peace . . . summons us, as disciples of Jesus Christ, to be peacemakers in our marriages, our homes, our friendships, our neighborhoods, our churches, our places of business and work, our country, and our world."[34] Making peace in a world bent on violence and death is not easy; in fact, it is impossible without the resources available to us in the Spirit. In the same sermon, Grounds told his audience that, "God has put at our disposal effective weapons for the waging of peace."[35] He went on to say that the Christian's ultimate weapon is prayer—"a weapon infinitely more powerful than all the guns and bayonets, tanks and planes, battleships and bombs of all the nations in all the world."[36]

In addition to urging God's people to pray for peace, preaching for *shalom* denounces acts of violence, from domestic abuse to homicide to genocide to war. Some issues are clearer than others. Torture, for example, has no place in the gospel, and therefore preachers should have no qualms denouncing such a practice from the pulpit, even if it implicates our own government. The same can be said of the genocide of whole peoples in places like Darfur in the Sudan and among the Karen people in Burma. These types of atrocities require prophetic preaching that openly confronts despotic governments, as well as inspires the church to engage in ministries of compassion, justice, and advocacy.

This type of preaching is dangerous as it inspires the redeemed in Christ to risk their lives; for often, the powers turn on peacemakers. This is the "sacrificial" part of peacemaking. For example, Christian Peacemaker Teams (CPT), an organization that applies "the same discipline and self-sacrifice to nonviolent peacemaking that armies devote to war," forms teams that "seek to follow God's Spirit as they work through local peacemakers who risk injury and death by waging nonviolent direct action to confront systems of violence and oppression."[37] The story of Tom Fox exemplifies the ultimate sacrifice of peacemaking. A CPT member working in Baghdad, Fox was abducted in November 2005 along with three other CPTers. While the other three were released after four months in captivity, Fox was not; he was shot dead and his body found on March 9, 2006.[38] Preaching for *shalom* aims to strengthen the church's commitment to peacemaking in a violent world no matter the cost. In light of the cross, which our Lord endured in order to show another way—a third way—can we preach anything less?

■ ■ ■

Theologian Ronald J. Sider's "Completely Pro-Life" exemplifies a *shalom* sermon. Based upon a definition of *shalom* as "fullness of life," the message calls us to respect life from womb to tomb. Whether you agree fully with his definition or not, how does the sermon cry out against destructive or violent practices? And how does it encourage life-affirming and peace-making ways?

NOTES

1. Lowell O. Erdahl, *Pro-Life/Pro-Peace: Life Affirming Alternatives to Abortion, War, Mercy-Killing and the Death Penalty* (Minneapolis: Augsburg, 1986), 14.
2. Cynthia Wedel, "Is Peace Controversial," in *Preaching on Peace*, eds. Ronald J. Sider and Darrel J. Brubaker (Philadelphia: Fortress, 1982), 18.
3. Joseph L. Bernardin, "A Consistent Ethic of Life," in *Seamless Garment*, ed. Thomas A. Nairn (Maryknoll, NY: Orbis, 2008), 7–20.
4. Ronald J. Sider, *Completely Pro-Life* (Downers Grove: IVP, 1986).
5. Even though the term has been attributed to Bishop Joseph L. Bernardin, it was actually coined by Eileen Egan, a member of the Catholic Worker and peace activist, in a 1971 interview. See M. Therese Lysaught, "From the Challenge of Peace to the Gift of Peace," in *The Consistent Ethic of Life*, ed. Thomas A. Nairn (Maryknoll, NY: Orbis, 2008), 112–13.
6. David Gushee, "The Consistent Ethic of Life," *Christian Ethics Today: Journal of Christian Ethics* 7/1 (February 2000).
7. Consistent Life Homepage, www.consistent-life.org/index.html (accessed 3 December 2010).
8. Sider, *Completely Pro-Life*, 11–31 (see esp. 15–16).
9. Quoted in Lysaught, "From the Challenge of Peace to the Gift of Peace," 114.
10. Walter Wink, *Engaging the Powers: Discernment and Resistance in a World of Domination* (Minneapolis: Fortress, 1992), 69.
11. Wink, *Engaging*, 69. Emphasis mine.
12. I would include in this list the violence to the unborn. For many, however, I recognize the violence of abortion is not readily apparent. To those who are interested in learning more about such violence, see "Types of Abortion Procedures," *American Pregnancy Association* www.americanpregnancy.org/unplannedpregnancy/abortionprocedures.html (accessed December 3, 2010).

13. Wink, *Engaging,* 175–93.
14. Alan Kreider, Eleanor Kreider, and Paulus Widjaja, *A Culture of Peace* (Intercourse, PA: Good Books, 2005), 16–17.
15. Erdahl, *Pro-Life/Pro-Peace,* 14.
16. Zac Niringiye, "In the Garden of Eden–I," *Journal of Latin American Theology* 5/1 (2010), 26.
17. Sider, *Completely Pro-Life,* 18.
18. David Gushee, "Opinion: Retrieving a Consistent Pro-Life Ethic," *Associated Baptist Press* (7 March 2007), www.abpnews.com/content/view/1950/120/ (accessed 12 December 2010).
19. Erdahl, *Pro-Life/Pro-Peace,* 24–28.
20. "Human Flourishing—A Thematic Overview," *InterVarsity,* www.intervarsity.org/gfm/download.php?id=6649&version_id=9219 (accessed December 10, 2010).
21. Vinay Samuel, "Mission as Transformation," *Transformation* 19/4 (October 2002), 244.
22. Samuel, "Mission as Transformation," 245–46. See also Al Tizon, *Transformation after Lausanne* (Oxford, et al: Regnum; Eugene, OR: Wipf & Stock, 2008), 145–147, where I go into more detail in interpreting Samuel's concept of personhood.
23. Erdahl, *Pro-Life/Pro-Peace,* 19.
24. Wink, *Engaging,* 175–86. I have hardly touched the surface of Wink's brilliant exegesis of these passages. For its full impact, one must read Wink's book, especially the pages listed here.
25. Wink, *Engaging,* 189–93.
26. Richard K. Taylor, *Love in Action: A Direct Action Handbook for Catholics Using Gospel Nonviolence to Reform and Renew the Church* (Philadelphia: R.K. Taylor, 2007), 16–20.
27. Eric Irivuzumugabe, *My Father, Maker of the Trees: How I Survived the Rwandan Genocide* (Grand Rapids: Baker, 2009). For a short article adapted from the book, see "Seventy Times Seven," *Prism* 17/1 (Jan/Feb 2010), 9–11.
28. This story can be found in Donald Kraybill, Steven Nolt, and David Weaver-Zercher, *Amish Grace* (San Francisco: Jossey-Bass, 2010).
29. Kristyn Komarnicki, "The Divine Logic of Forgiveness," *Prism* 17/1 (January/February 2010), 2.
30. Martin Luther King Jr. *Strength to Love* (New York: Pocket Books, 1968), 43.
31. Gushee, "Opinion."
32. Gushee, "Opinion."
33. Kreider, Kreider, and Widjaja, *Culture of Peace,* 111.
34. Vernon C. Grounds, "Spiritual Weapons for Waging Peace," in *Preaching on Peace,* eds. Ronald J. Sider and Darrel J. Brubaker (Philadelphia: Fortress, 1982), 62.
35. Grounds, "Spiritual Weapons," 63.
36. Grounds, "Spiritual Weapons," 64.

37. "Mission Statement," *Christian Peacemaker Teams,* www.cpt.org/about/
mission (accessed December 13, 2010).

38. "U.S. Hostage in Iraq Confirmed Dead," *BBC News* (March 11, 2006),
http://news.bbc.co.uk/2/hi/middle_east/4795678.stm (accessed December 13, 2010).

Completely Pro-Life

■ ■ ■

Ronald J. Sider
GENESIS 1–2

Everyone supports life. But some funny inconsistencies pop up on the way to its practical protection.

Why do many liberal and radical activists champion nuclear disarmament to protect the sanctity of human life and then defend the destruction of 1.5 million unborn American babies each year? Are "sexual freedom" and affluent lifestyles finally more important than helpless, inconvenient babies?

Why do the members of the National Right to Life Committee (a major anti-abortion group) score far lower on other pro-life issues, such as opposition to the arms race, handgun control, and concern for the poor, than do the members of the National Abortion Rights Action League (a pro-abortion group)? Don't missiles, handguns, and poverty also destroy human beings?

Got a problem pregnancy? Abort the child.

Arrest a murderer? Fry him.

Dislike another country? Bomb it.

Feel insecure? Build another missile.

Bothered by a sick relative? Yank the plug.[1]

What does it really mean to be pro-life? The answer, of course, depends on one's basic values. If one endorses Marx's philosophical materialism, then sacrificing millions of people on the way to a secular utopia is not inconsistent. If one believes that the fetus is merely a physical appendage of the mother and not an independent human life, then favoring abortion is not inconsistent. If freedom is a higher value than justice, then majoring on religious and political liberty even at the expense of a decent life or even life itself for the poor is not inconsistent. Whether consciously or subconsciously, everyone's definition of what it means to be "pro-life" emerges from his or her deepest beliefs. I seek to ground my definition of what it means to be pro-life in my understanding of what the Bible says about life.

The opening chapters of Genesis sketch a glorious picture of the fullness of life intended for humanity by the Creator. A harmony of right relationships prevails everywhere—with God, with one another, and with the earth. Although it is not used here, the Hebrew word *shalom* is perhaps the best word to signify this fullness of life enjoyed as Adam and Eve walked in obedient relationship with God and in responsible stewardship over God's garden. Sin, however, shattered this *shalom* and disrupted relationships with God, neighbor, and earth. But God refused to abandon us. Beginning with Abraham, God called out a special people to be his instruments of revelation and salvation for all. Through Moses and the prophets, the judges and the writers of wisdom, God patiently showed this chosen people how to live the abundant life.

As in the garden, God said that *shalom* starts with a right relationship with God. But it also includes right relationships with the neighbor: economic justice, respect for all persons including a special concern for the poor and weak, faithful family life, fair courts, and, of course, an end to war. Starkly, Moses clarified the options at the end of Deuteronomy. Life in every sense would follow if Israel obeyed God's commands, death and evil if they disobeyed. "I call heaven and earth to witness against you this day that I have set before you life and death . . . . Choose life so that you and your descendants may live" (Deut. 30:19).

They chose death. Worshipping idols and oppressing the poor, they defied the Author of Life. Still God would not give up. God's prophets looked ahead to a time when the Messiah would come to restore life and *shalom*. And in Christ, we received abundant life. "I came that they may have life, and have it abundantly" (John 10:10).

Increasingly since the Enlightenment, however, secular thinkers have promoted purely human paths to wholeness of life. If only we will offer quality education to all; if only we will modify our social environment; if only we will change the economic system; if only we will undertake this or that bit of human engineering, secular thinkers promise a new person and a new social order freed from the stupidity and selfishness of the past. The Marxist promise that utopia follows the abolition of private property is merely one of the more naïve versions of the Enlightenment's secular humanism.

Christians know this is dangerous nonsense. Certainly we can and should affect significant changes by improving social structures. But no amount of social engineering will create unselfish persons. Tragically, the human problem lies far deeper than mere (even very unjust) social systems. It lies in the proud, rebellious, self-centered heart of every person. A transforming relationship with the living God is the only way to heal the brokenness at the core of our being.

That is why Jesus told Nicodemus that he must be born again (John 3:1-21). It is only as we believe that God has sent his only Son to live and die for us that we experience genuine life—indeed eternal life (John 3:16). As the Gospel of John says so beautifully and powerfully, eternal life begins now as we believe in Christ because, "This is eternal life, that they may know you, the only true God, and Jesus Christ whom you have sent" (17:3). As the Spirit begins to transform believers, we enjoy the first fruits of eternal life even now. We can enjoy an abundant life here and now, as we live in Christ and are reshaped according to the pattern of his perfection.

But even the *shalom* of abundant Christian living pales by comparison with the glorious life of the age to come. "For me to live is Christ and to die is gain" was Paul's confident cry (Phil. 1:21, KJV; cf. Acts 20:24). To be pro-life does not mean that physical human life is the highest value. There are many things worth dying for. To say that I or another Christian opposes the nuclear arms race because human life is exceedingly precious is not to say that life here on earth is the ultimate good. "Thy lovingkindness is better than life," the psalmist exclaimed (63:3, KJV). Jesus taught that we should sacrifice eyes, limbs, possessions, indeed even life itself for the sake of the kingdom of God and the harmony of right relationships that make up the righteousness of that kingdom (Matt. 18:7-9; also 6:25-34; Luke 12:13-31). Because Christians know that Jesus is the resurrection and the life (John 11:25), Christians will sacrifice their own physical lives for freedom, justice, peace, and evangelism. Jesus has conquered death in all its terror. Therefore, we know that death is only a temporary transition to life even more abundant.

But this biblical teaching about eternal life does not refer to some ethereal, spiritual fairyland totally unrelated to human history and the created order. Paul clearly teaches that *this* groaning creation will be freed of its bondage and decay and experience the glorious liberty of the children of God (Rom. 8:18-25). He also describes God's cosmic plan of transformation to restore all things in both heaven and earth to their original wholeness and shalom (Col. 1:15-20). God intends to transform all that is good in human culture, purify it of all sinful distortion, and make it a part of the abundant life of the eternal kingdom.

Until Christ's return, all attempts to realize that fullness of life in American society, and all other societies, will have dreadfully imperfect results. But history demonstrates that it is possible to combat racism, end slavery, and foster democracy. We could end the formidable evil of abortion. We can erect signs of that coming kingdom both in church and in the larger society. To be consistently pro-life is to allow our thoughts and actions to be shaped by the full biblical picture of life-abundant, the wholeness God established at creation and will finally restore at the Second Coming. And that means that biblical norms rather than secular ideologies must set our agenda. I have absolutely no commitment to ideologies of left or right. I have only one commitment—to Jesus Christ and God's revealed Word.

That means two key things for my politics. First, it means I would like my stand on every political issue to be grounded in biblical norms. Now I know I don't accomplish that fully, but I'd like to. And I also know how important it is to do careful socioeconomic research because every political choice combines value judgments and complex factual analysis. But when it comes to the norms that guide my politics, I want them to come from God's Word, not Karl Marx, Adam Smith, or Eastern monism.

Letting the full biblical picture guide my politics means something else as well. It means letting God's Word shape the balance of my political agenda. It is not hard to find people who argue that abortion is the most important political issue. Others a few years ago said the same thing about nuclear weapons. Others say the same thing about world hunger or economic injustice or the environment. Who is right?

Part of the way to answer that question is to ask, "What does the Creator of Life care about?" I want the balance of my political agenda to be shaped by the balance of things that the Bible says are important to the Author of Life. That, it seems to me, demands that we say no to abortion and the nuclear arms race, as well as no to murder by environmental pollution, economic oppression, and euthanasia.

If aborting millions of unborn children each year is wrong, then walking down a path that increases the likelihood of the ultimate abortion—where a nuclear exchange obliterates hundreds of millions of people—is also wrong. If human life is precious, then it is a terrible sin to stand idly by in suffocating affluence when we could prevent the death by malnutrition and starvation of 12 million children each year. And yet some Christians urge us to focus all or most of our attention on combating abortion and to relegate economic justice to the category of the less urgent. I cannot see how that is a consistent pro-life stance.

Nor does the list of consistently pro-life issues end with abortion, the nuclear arms race, and poverty. Three hundred fifty thousand persons in the United States alone die prematurely each year because of smoking. The global death toll from cigarettes already runs in the tens of millions, and some of those cigarettes come from here. Alcoholism enslaves 10 million Americans. Their personal tragedies entangle another 30 million family members, close friends, and co-workers in a hell of crippling car accidents, fires, lost productivity, and damaged health, with an economic cost to the nation of $120 billion annually. Racism in India, South Africa, and South Philadelphia maims and kills. So does the rape of our environment. Every day, erosion and construction remove enough productive land to feed 260,000 people for a year. In a world of hunger and starvation, that is a pro-life issue. In short, if biblical norms set the Christian's agenda, then we will reject one-issue approaches in favor of a commitment to all that is of concern to the Author of Life.

The media often paints all pro-life people as reactionary, one-issue folk who act as if life begins at conception and ends at birth. That's a nasty smear. But the best way to disprove it is to adopt a consistently pro-life approach and demonstrate that we care both about the unborn child and the poor mother struggling to care for another child; that we care both about the unborn child and the millions of starving children already born. In short, precisely because human life is created in the image of God, we care about the fullness of human life from womb to tomb—and therefore we care about peace and justice and freedom and a wholesome environment.

What does it mean to be pro-life? It means letting the Author of Life set our agenda. It means saying no to right-wing ideological agendas that make freedom, family, and the crusade against abortion more important than justice and nuclear disarmament. It means saying no to left-wing ideological agendas that do the reverse. It means letting the balance of biblical concerns set the priorities for our political engagement.

Championing a completely pro-life agenda will likely produce harsh attack from both the left and the right. One side will attack us for our stance on the poor and capital punishment, and the other side for our defense of the unborn. Being willing to be the target for both left-wing and right-wing ideological attack is the price Christians must pay for biblical faithfulness today.

The acid test of the integrity of the Christian pro-life movement in this generation will be whether we have the courage to let the Author of Life, rather than competing secular ideologies, shape our agenda.

NOTE

1. Source unknown.

Ronald J. Sider is professor of theology, holistic ministry, and public policy at Palmer Theological Seminary of Eastern University in Wynnewood, Pennsylvania. He is also founder and president of Evangelicals for Social Action. His many books include the enduring *Rich Christians in an Age of Hunger, Completely Pro-Life, Just Generosity,* and *The Scandal of the Evangelical Conscience.*

CHAPTER 10

PREACHING THE
Scandal of Jesus

I often describe the Graduate Theological Union (GTU), where I had the privilege of studying, as arguably the most diverse, liberal, theological institution on the planet. Located in Berkeley, California (or "Berserk-ley" as some prefer to call it), the GTU is a partnership of nine mainline Protestant and Catholic seminaries, and also includes centers for Jewish, Buddhist, and Islamic studies (as well as many other centers, including one for gay-lesbian studies in one of the member seminaries). As if that is not theologically and ideologically diverse enough, the GTU also has a cooperative relationship with the University of California, Berkeley—once the center of radical student movements and American-Marxist intellectualism—offering joint degrees together. The city of Berkeley itself is a laboratory for many homespun religious experiments; devotees of so-called New Age movements feel at home there, as do practitioners of pagan religions such as Wicca and the occult.

It is in this religious, radical-secular milieu in which the GTU marinates. And as a result, it offers a theological education like no other in the world, as it forces students to look through a pluralist lens of traditional and non-traditional religions, as well as the "religions" of secular humanism, intellectualism, and spiritual cynicism. An evangelical missionary-type like me, progressive as I may or may not be, had no business being there! At least that's what a handful of my fellow evangelicals told me.

But why not? Rather than living up to the reputation that we evangelicals are intolerant, theologically inflexible, and intellectually dishonest, I ran into the fray called the GTU and experienced what I consider to be the best theological education one could have. I admit it was not always easy. If a marginalized group exists at the GTU, it would be the evangelicals. During an especially discouraging time, I remember sitting in the office of GTU President James Donahue who said something that captures a truly ecumenical spirit. After apologizing on behalf of the GTU for sometimes marginalizing evangelicals, he said something like, "Al, the GTU will have succeeded if you come out of here a better evangelical."

I chewed on this for quite a while and began to understand that true ecumenism does not consist of a melting pot where all religious convictions are watered-down into a bland, gray soup. If it does, then all the hoopla concerning diversity and interfaith relations would be meaningless and useless. True ecumenism acknowledges and appreciates the rich diversity of the world's religions but encourages people of different faiths to *be* who they are so that genuine dialogue can occur. Far from avoiding differences that may offend, true ecumenism cultivates a sacred space where people of different faiths can intensely, passionately, and respectfully listen to and share their heartfelt convictions with one another. In this light, Christians should bring to the ecumenical round table nothing less than the beliefs and practices of authentic biblical Christianity.

Of course, only theological elites and scholars are invited to "round tables." What does ecumenism have to do with the real world of ordinary people? The truth is, the real world is itself becoming "a round table," as the cultures and religions of the world are converging like never before. Indeed increasingly diverse people of the world find themselves living in the same neighborhoods, shopping in the same stores, eating in the same restaurants, and sending their children to the same schools. In a rapidly globalizing world, the church is forced to acknowledge the religio-cultural diversity that makes up the human family.

Missional preachers know this, and we do our part in equipping God's people to be faithful to the gospel, even as we take seriously and respectfully the many religions of the world. We do this by preaching nothing less than what theologian Vinoth Ramachandra calls "the scandal of Jesus."[1] What Jesus embodied in his birth, life, teachings, death, and resurrection—the good news of the kingdom—was and is scandalous, for it claims the uniqueness and universality of Christ, over and against the all-roads-lead-to-God theologies, which have gained momentum of postmodern proportions in both academic and church circles. Naturally, this theological orientation disdains any exclusivist claims on the part of any religion. So, for example, the claim that Jesus' statement that he is *the* way, *the* truth, and *the* life (John 14:6) represents an exclusive means to salvation and a singular path to God for all people is summarily dismissed, ridiculed, and even met with hostility. Theologian Ken Gnanakan calls this dilemma "the pluralistic predicament."[2]

The Pluralistic Predicament

How can the people of God affirm the uniqueness and universality of Christ without being obnoxious about it—scandalous, but not obnoxious? Or, to ask it more properly, how can Christians be faithfully Christian in a pluralistic world? Three broad approaches frame what academics call a "theology of religions": pluralism, inclusivism, and exclusivism.[3] We would do well to gain a basic understanding of each.

Pluralism

Pluralism refers to a school of thought that views Christianity as but one among many valid ways to salvation. Gnanakan makes an important distinction between recognizing a *plurality* of religions— which is simply a fact of existence—and affirming religious *pluralism*—which validates every religion as pointing to a transcendent reality called God in its own culturally conditioned, traditionally specific way.[4] Pluralists assert that God cannot be contained in any one religion; in fact, they hold out the possibility that every religion may contain a piece or two of the grand puzzle of Truth. In this thinking, Christ is not *the* way, but *a* way to salvation. Theologian Paul Knitter claims that Jesus maintained his uniqueness "by [his] ability to relate to—that is, to include and be included by—other unique religious figures." He goes on to say that "such an understanding of Jesus views him not as exclusive or even as normative but as theocentric, as a universally relevant manifestation of divine revelation and salvation."[5] It is this "theocentric perspective"—i.e., the God whom religion cannot contain as the starting point for reflection—that enables Knitter and other pluralists to reason in this way.

I confess that I find pluralism appealing. First of all, would it not be easier in a world that includes a plurality of religions? But it is not just because pluralism is more convenient; I want to affirm the intent of pluralists to live harmoniously amongst neighbors of other religions. As Gnanakan notes, "The strength of the pluralistic position is its forceful reminder of the urgent need for us to become an integral part of the global community."[6]

However, although I find biblical warrant for living harmoniously with others (a far more biblical teaching than to kill one another in the name of religion!), I am hard-pressed to find that same warrant for the pluralistic position itself. Pluralists such as the aforementioned Knitter and prominent Asian theologians such as Stanley Samartha, Aloysius Pieris, and Raimundo Panikkar do argue from Scripture. But for me, their arguments ultimately fall flat as their hermeneutics rely too heavily on liberal, modernist lenses.[7] For example, Knitter sidesteps exclusive claims in the New Testament by saying that they reflect the writers' later notions more than the core message of Jesus.[8] Through faulty hermeneutics, pluralists lead us astray as their thinking inevitably diminishes the personal knowability of God, the ultimate relevance of the cross of Christ, and the importance of mission and evangelization. These and other reasons cause many biblical theologians such as Christopher Wright to conclude, "It is highly questionable whether pluralism can be regarded as a valid option for Christian theology of religions."[9]

Inclusivism

Inclusivism contends that Christianity is the overall framework for religious truth, yet other religions are generously accommodated within that framework. Since all truth is God's truth, and since Christ is "the truth," then Christ can be found in one way or another in all religions.[10] Karl Rahner's famous idea of the "anonymous Christian" represents this school well.[11] I like Wright's explanation of Rahner's idea; he writes, "Those who genuinely respond to God's grace as experienced in another religion are implicitly responding to Christ and may therefore be called 'anonymous Christians.' They will be saved by Christ, but through the 'sacraments' of their own religion, unless and until they are confronted with the gospel."[12] Rahner was a theologian, not an evangelist. So we can surmise that, for him, the

language of "anonymous Christian" was not for evangelistic purposes, for telling adherents of other religions that they are followers
of Christ whether they know it or not. Instead, it was primarily for
theological purposes, pointing to the possibility of salvation outside
of Christianity but not outside of Christ.

In contrast to pluralism, which views the validity of all religions
on their own merits, the inclusivist position approaches the pluralistic predicament by trying to hold in tension the centrality of Christ
and the value of other religions. This is commendable, and if we can
truly and tightly hold this tension in place, then we might accept
Gnanakan's statement that inclusivism "may be a justifiable position
for even evangelicals to consider."[13] But one of the dangers is precisely our inability to keep this tension in place, thereby leading both
preachers and the congregations under our charge along the pluralist
path. "The inclusivist," Gnanakan posits, "could really be an 'anonymous' pluralist"; that is, accept the validity of other religions for
salvation without even knowing it![14] Moreover, I am certain that adherents of other religions would be appalled to learn that we consider
them Christians "behind their backs"; at that point dialogue or any
kind of honest exchange would cease. So as appealing as inclusivism
may be, I do not believe it ultimately serves the *missio Dei*.

Exclusivism

The last broad school of thought to consider here is exclusivism,
which views the uniqueness and universality of Christ in the strictest
sense. That is, exclusivism holds that Jesus Christ, as he is uniquely
described in the New Testament, is the only way of salvation for all
people, and that Christianity, however imperfect, is the only legiti-
mate means through which people can come to true faith. By implication then, all other religions are at best inadequate and, at worst,
demonic deceptions. This is an exclusivist theology of religions, and
most evangelicals would fall squarely in this camp. Knitter in fact
calls it "the conservative evangelical model."[15]

Traditionally, exclusivists have had the easiest time finding biblical support for their position, not just in specific passages, such as
John 14:6 and Acts 4:12, but in the whole of the biblical story, which
tells of God's self-revelation in the formation of Israel as a light to
the nations and then in the person of Jesus as Savior of the world, to

whom every person will bow and every tongue confess (Isa. 45:23; Rom. 14:11; Phil. 2:10). To read the biblical story differently, i.e., to read the Bible as saying that Yahweh God who became flesh in Jesus Christ is but one of many ways to attain salvation, would require either a low view of biblical authority or hermeneutical gymnastics, or perhaps a little of both. Exclusivists affirm that the Bible proclaims nothing less than the uniqueness of Jesus Christ as the crucified and risen Lord. As such, Jesus Christ is the way of salvation for all.

And yet, there is something off-putting and insensitive about strict ideological exclusivism, as exclusivists dismiss wholesale all truth claims of other religions while failing to take the log out of their own eye. For example, an exclusivistic orientation undeniably did its part in the travesty of the colonial project throughout the world. Priests and missionaries of the "one true religion" sailed along with invaders, violently imposing Christianity on whole peoples. If Christianity is the only way, they reasoned, then the natives need to be saved by hook or by crook. They will thank us later. As biblically grounded as the exclusivist position may be, colonial Christianity and other insensitive, disrespectful, arrogant products of ideological exclusivism are decidedly unbiblical.

The Scandal of Jesus

So what are disciples of Christ—people of the Way—to do amid this pluralistic predicament? Should we: (1) accommodate the all-roads-lead-to-God theology of the pluralists, (2) impose a Christian framework upon our friends of other faiths like the inclusivists, or (3) insensitively dismiss all truth claims of other faiths that do not conform to our understanding of the Bible like the exclusivists? I find these choices inadequate. I opt instead to affirm and practice a fourth option: "the scandal of Jesus."

The scandal of Jesus has at least two dimensions—the scandal of particularity and the scandal of universal love.[16] To preach Jesus as the way, the truth, and the life is indeed scandalous in a pluralistic world that summarily dismisses all claims of absolute truth. In this aspect, we identify with exclusivists and are willing to take the heat for it. Ramachandra notes that "this gospel has been the cause of offense from the very beginnings of the Christian movement."[17] Unless we are willing to question the integrity of the biblical message, we are compelled to proclaim Jesus of Nazareth as the Savior of the world.

Moreover, for Christians, to affirm Jesus as Savior assumes the most honest posture, and thus holds the most potential for real dialogue with other religions. Admittedly, it also holds the most potential for confrontation and therefore conflict; which is why this commitment to gospel particularity needs to be balanced with a commitment to an equally true dimension of the gospel—namely, the scandal of universal love.

Ironically, one of the distinctions of the particular message of the gospel is not God's limited blessings for a particular people, but unconditional, universal love for all. Jesus' association with the lowly, the poor, the leper, the sinner, the Gentile, the Samaritan—people whom ancient mainstream Jewish society had shunned—sent a clear message, which reverberates through time and beyond cultures, and it is this: No one is outside the purview of God's vision of redemption. This biblical, historical Jesus of Nazareth, the Christ for all time, loves all, and this message differentiates him from all the others.[18]

This scandal of universal love (which, by the way, is not discontinuous with the Old Testament, especially as one considers the story of Jonah) has fundamental implications for how we understand people of other faiths. First, it leaves no room for self-righteous arrogance about being God's chosen people. Second, it leaves no room for the church to decide "who's in and who's out." This is God's sole domain. And third, it leaves plenty of room for God's redemptive activity to go beyond the religious establishment, that is, beyond the airtight doctrines of official Christianity. With this statement, I am not saying that people can be saved through any religion, as inclusivists would hold, but that God's radical love transcends the establishment; it transcends human-drawn lines in the sand. Just ask Jonah regarding the Ninevites or the first-century Jews regarding Samaritans and Gentiles! "Scandalous Christians" proclaim the Jesus of the New Testament, and as an outflow of that, we extend the indiscriminate love of God toward all—including those considered anathema—in Jerusalem, in Judea and Samaria, and to the ends of the earth (Acts 1:8).

The interreligious relationship poses complex issues, and I am certain my understanding of the scandal of Jesus needs further development. There is enough here, however, to propose at least three practical postures of Christians impacted by the scandal of the gospel in a pluralistic world.

Christian Hospitality

First, "scandalous Christians" reflect the hospitality of God—yes, in traditionally understood ways toward people in general, but also in far-reaching ways toward people of other faiths. Christian hospitality is basically extending toward others what we ourselves have experienced of God's welcoming spirit to become a part of God's family. This hospitality must extend to people of other faiths. Theologian Amos Yong has made a compelling case for understanding the church's global mission in terms of this kind of hospitality. He writes, "The Christian mission is nothing more or less than our participation in the hospitality of God. God is not only the principal 'missionary' but also the host of all creation who invites the world to 'God's banquet of salvation.'"[19] To the degree that we extend hospitality as graciously as God has extended it to us, we participate in God's mission.

Among its practical implications, Christian hospitality means to practice openness toward people of other faiths, that is, to relate to "the other" not with the agenda to convert so much as to befriend, to listen, and to learn, even as we maintain our Christian identity uncompromisingly and unashamedly. I have described here nothing less than developing friendships with Muslims, Buddhists, Hindus, and person of other faiths. How wonderfully scandalous it would be, for example, to cultivate a friendship with a Muslim today in a world that seems hell-bent toward yet another tragic Muslim-Christian bloodbath. Scandalous Christians befriend and are willing to be befriended by people of other faiths.

Authentic Dialogue

Christian hospitality paves the way for authentic interreligious dialogue, the second practical posture of scandalous Christians. As we established earlier, authentic dialogue can occur only if each party stays true to his or her identity. For Christians, this means coming to interreligious encounters as followers of Christ and affirming nothing less than the Jesus of the Gospels, but we do this in the context of God's hospitality. This means that we also come with the openness to learn and to be enriched, challenged, and changed by "the other."

I am not overlooking the vulnerability and the risk of this posture, for if we hold out the possibility of our dialogue partner coming to faith in Christ, then the rules of mutuality and authenticity also hold out the possibility of our being changed by virtue of our conversation partner's religious convictions. But is not this kind of risk part and parcel of what it means to love our neighbors as ourselves—or has someone come up with a way to love our neighbors without extending respect and dignity to them? I for one would not feel very loved if a person of another faith engaged me in a one-way monologue about his or her faith and did not give me the space to share my heart and mind about the things of God. If I am going to love my neighbor as myself, I must listen, learn, and be vulnerable. I am convinced that this kind of posture is essential to pave the way for authentic dialogue.

Humanitarian Partnership

Third, and also flowing out of Christian hospitality, is the practical posture of humanitarian partnership. With God's indiscriminate compassion and justice in mind, scandalous Christians hold hands with any and all who work toward peace and justice in the world. This kind of partnership not only models a much-needed alternative to the animosity, conflict, and bloodshed that often exist between religions; it also joins forces to accomplish God's vision for peace and justice.

For example, theologian Melba Maggay recalls when Filipino evangelicals during the People Power Revolution of 1986 experienced "a crisis of paradigm." As Catholics, Protestants, Muslims, and other worshipers were called upon to pray that justice prevail, some fellow evangelicals asked Maggay, "What shall we do?" to which she replied, "Let's kneel!"[20] Linking arms, or in Maggay's case, kneeling down together with people of other faiths, to help victims of a catastrophe or pass just legislation or protest war or advocate for an oppressed people attests both to God's unconditional love and God's commitment to peace and justice for all. Christian peace and justice activist Ann Miller pleads with us all: "Christian, Muslim, Hindu, atheist, Jew—we can all help to create a more loving nation and world."[21]

Preaching the Scandal of Jesus

Missional preaching strives to form scandalous Christians in a pluralistic world, and the following three summary principles can guide our proclamation accordingly.

Biblical Jesus

First and foremost, we preach Jesus as he is presented to us in the New Testament. As Ramachandra notes, there are many "Jesuses" presented in the various theologies of religions available to us, but we would be less than the church of Jesus Christ if we did not continue to affirm the Jesus to whom the New Testament definitively testifies.[22] Far from being simply a naïve position, this conviction is rooted in critical scholarship conducted by respected biblical theologians like Jurgen Moltmann, N. T. Wright, Ken Gnanakan, and Vinoth Ramachandra.[23] Space and time will not allow me to interact with their respective brilliant works here (although I do quote Gnanakan and Ramachandra extensively in this chapter). Suffice it say that "unless we are prepared to be totally skeptical about the historical value of these narratives [the Gospels in particular], these remain the principal source of testimony concerning Jesus of Nazareth."[24] Missional preachers preach the holy offense—the scandal—of the gospel as presented in the Gospels and the rest of the New Testament, and thus equip God's people to be at once both uncompromising in biblical faith and loving in action.

Personal Jesus

We also preach the God who can be known personally in Jesus Christ; we preach the person of Jesus over the doctrines concerning Jesus; we preach Christ over the religion of Christianity. There is a difference! And missional preachers have an acute awareness of this. This awareness enables us to celebrate the perfection of Christ over and against the imperfections we have constructed around him—i.e., the limitations of the church's creeds, doctrines, and practices. Try as we might to build an airtight, error-proof religious system, the church's words, symbols, and practices do not fully convey the reality of God, the person of Jesus, and the presence of the Spirit, all of which welcome personal encounter. The Christian faith is first and foremost a personal one; it is a relationship with the living God through Jesus Christ. The famed missionary E. Stanley Jones tried to convey why the personal nature of God is essential:

> "Why won't principles do? Why do we need a personal God?" someone asks. Well, suppose you go to a child crying for its mother and say, "Don't cry, little child; I'm giving to you the principle of

motherhood." Would the tears dry and the face light up? Hardly. The child would brush aside your principle of motherhood and cry for its mother. We all want, not a principle nor a picture, but a Person.[25]

Missional preachers do not lose sight of the object of our faith, which is not a body of doctrine, not a great philosophy, not a high moral ideal, but a person—the person of Jesus who can be known and experienced today by the presence of the Holy Spirit.

Confident Gospel Relationships

We preach to instill confidence in the name of Jesus. To preach anything less than the biblical, personal Jesus—say, the Jesus who is one among many great spiritual leaders (pluralism), or the Jesus hidden in the ideas of other religions (inclusivism), or the Jesus who belittles and dismisses people because they don't believe correctly (exclusivism)—only weakens confidence in the Name and in the power of the gospel. Missional preachers, on the other hand, strive to form confident Christians who can declare with Paul, "I am not ashamed of the gospel; it is the power of God for salvation to everyone who has faith" (Rom. 1:16).

At the same time, we preach genuine (read, nonmanipulative) relationship-building with our Muslim, Buddhist, Hindu, New Age, atheist, and all other neighbors. We preach Christian hospitality, which, as we have seen, means relational openness that leads to dialogue and humanitarian partnership. In light of the confidence in the gospel to which we are called, missional preachers encourage and equip God's people to form genuine friendships across religious lines. For as church consultant Jim Henderson discovered, "When people like each other, the rules change."[26] Missional preachers help God's people change the rules of engagement with people of other faiths via genuine relationship-building. We help followers of Jesus unlearn the unbending, impersonal, and often manipulative ways of traditional apologetics, and rediscover the lost art of "conversational God-talk" that flows from genuine relationships.

■ ■ ■

To end Part Two with the scandal of Jesus was no accident, for although I have identified the scandal with preaching the uniqueness and universality of Christ in a pluralistic world, the truth is, preaching for the purpose of accomplishing all seven missional goals is scandalous through and through.

In "Joining Jesus on an Excursion beyond Ancient Borders," pastor and theologian Tony Richie delivers a "scandalous sermon," as he mines the rich story of Jesus' journey through Gentile territory. How does the sermon show respect to people of other cultures and other faiths, while lifting up the unique name of Jesus?

NOTES

1. Vinoth Ramachandra, *The Recovery of Mission* (Delhi, India: ISPCK, 1996), 179–216.
2. Ken Gnanakan, *The Pluralistic Predicament* (Bangalore, India: TBT, 1992), 1–21.
3. Christopher J. H. Wright, "Theology of Religions," *Evangelical Dictionary of World Missions,* ed. A. Scott Moreau (Grand Rapids: Baker; Carlisle, Cumbria, UK: Paternoster, 2000), 951.
4. Gnanakan, *Pluralistic Predicament,* 1–2. See also Wright, "Theology of Religions," 953.
5. Paul F. Knitter, *No Other Name? A Critical Survey of Christian Attitudes Toward the World Religions* Philippines edition (Quezon City, Philippines: Claretian, 1985), 171–72.
6. Gnanakan, *Pluralistic Predicament,* 119.
7. See Parts I and II of Ramachandra, *Recovery of Mission,* 3–176.
8. Knitter, *No Other Name?* 182–86.
9. Wright, "Theology of Religions," 953.
10. Wright, "Theology of Religions," 952.
11. Karl Rahner, "Christianity and World Religions," in *The Content of Faith: The Best of Karl Rahner's Theological Writings,* eds. Karl Lehmann and Albert Raffelt, trans. Harvey D. Egan (New York: Crossroad, 1993), 51–55. See also Joseph H. Wong, "Anonymous Christians: Karl Rahner's Pneuma-Christocentrism and an East-West Dialogue," *Theological Studies* 55/4 (1994), 609–37.
12. Wright, "Theology of Religions," 952.
13. Gnanakan, *Pluralistic Predicament,* 93.
14. Gnanakan, *Pluralistic Predicament,* 94.
15. Knitter, *No Other Name?* 75–96; Gnanakan, *Pluralistic Predicament,* 24–25.
16. These two dimensions roughly reflect Part III of Ramachandra's *Recovery of Mission* (pp. 179–284) where he talks first of the uniqueness of Jesus in chapter 6 and the universal mission of the gospel in chapters 7 and 8.
17. Ramachandra, *Recovery of Mission,* 188.
18. Gnanakan, *Pluralistic Predicament,* 46.

19. Amos Yong, *Hospitality & the Other: Pentecost, Christian Practices, and the Neighbor* (Maryknoll, NY: Orbis, 2008), 131.
20. Melba Maggay, "Signs of the Presence of the Kingdom in the February Revolution," in *Toward a Theology of People Power,* ed. Douglas J. Elwood (Quezon City, Philippines: New Day, 1988), 64.
21. Ann Miller, "New Year's Revolutions," *The Huffington Post* (December 31, 2010), www.huffingtonpost.com/ann-miller/new-years-revolutions_b_802974.html (accessed December 31, 2010).
22. Ramachandra, *Recovery of Mission,* 182–87.
23. I have cited Gnanakan and Ramachandra extensively in this chapter. As for the other two, see Jurgen Moltmann, *The Way of Jesus Christ: Christology in Messianic Dimensions* (San Francisco: Harper and Row, 1990) and N. T. Wright, *The Challenge of Jesus: Rediscovering Who Jesus Was and Is* (Downers Grove: IVP Academic, 1999).
24. Ramachandra, *Recovery of Mission,* 183.
25. E. Stanley Jones, *Abundant Living* (New York and Nashville: Abingdon-Cokesbury, 1942), 371.
26. Jim Henderson and Matt Casper, *Jim and Casper Go to Church: Frank Conversations about Faith, Churches, and Well-Meaning Christians* (Carol Stream, IL: Barna Group/Tyndale House, 2007), xvi.

Joining Jesus on an Excursion beyond Ancient Borders

■ ■ ■

Tony Richie
MARK 7:24-30

When I became a Christian more than thirty years ago, I struggled to understand the reality of so many religions in the world. Perhaps you have also thought about that? However, I was and am completely convinced of the absolute truth and power of the gospel of Jesus Christ. I hope you are, too. What indescribable peace has filled my life since trusting in Jesus as my personal Lord and Savior. Hallelujah!

Later, when I responded to God's calling to preach and to pastor, I didn't expect to encounter so many people of non-Christian faiths. In my second pastorate a woman in our church, a local schoolteacher, married a Muslim man originally from Egypt. To be candid, I tried to stop this interfaith relationship, quoting 2 Corinthians 6:14-16 for support. I was unsuccessful. And he came to church with her. He came to church fellowship functions, too. I was almost forced to get acquainted. I discovered he was gracious and polite—and very interested in discussing not only his own faith but Christianity as well.

Later, in my fourth pastorate, there was a Buddhist man whose wife had converted to Christ. Out of commitment to their marriage, he regularly attended our church with her. In this same congregation was an African American man, formerly a member of the Nation of Islam; he finally converted to Christ through the lifelong witness of his grandmother. In each of these cases, I think it's safe to say that we all experienced mutual understanding and enrichment. As for myself, I sincerely sought to share Christ's love to God's glory.

A few years ago I was part of a more formal interreligious meeting in Rome, Italy. Catholics and Protestants met with representatives of other world religions, including Buddhism, Hinduism, Islam, Judaism, and an African indigenous religion, Yoruba. We engaged in dialogue concerning the dynamics of Christian mission and evangelism in religiously pluralistic settings. I was honored to share an evangelical voice in the conversation, and I was pleasantly surprised at how well it was heard. Sadly, that distinctive evangelical voice is sometimes not heard because it's not even spoken in such gatherings. Why? Because evangelicals are often absent and uninvolved due to our own misguided reluctance to join Jesus on an excursion beyond the borders of our own comfortable group.

In our text, Jesus, in his search for privacy, left the plains of Gennesaret, and proceeded northward to a region that had as its metropolitan center the ancient pagan city of Tyre. Jesus entered a Hellenistic environment. This was, apparently, Jesus' only excursion beyond the ancient borders of Israel. He immediately encountered Gentiles who'd heard stories of his power but had experienced no previous direct contact with him. They came looking for help, especially healing. Prominent among these was a Syrophoenician woman who sought an exorcism for her suffering daughter. She was an outsider not only geographically but also culturally; she was a female and a foreigner from a vastly different faith background. But, she evidenced a firm, if uninformed, faith in God. Although initially reticent, Jesus eventually carried on a surprising dialogue with her. Explaining that neither she nor her people were presently part of the covenant people, Jesus nevertheless allowed her to experience an advance benefit. Her daughter was dramatically healed and delivered!

Evangelical Christians today can and should join Jesus on an excursion beyond ancient borders. While reaffirming the uniquely distinctive work of God in and through the people of the new covenant, let us search out seekers beyond the Christian church. Like Jesus, we may recognize faith, including uninformed or ill-informed faith, wherever we find it, and respond to it with honest dialogue and powerful prayer for God's healing action.

Brothers and sisters in Christ, we can no longer afford to indulge in denial. Religious plurality, in the sense of various faiths existing side by side, is a fact of life. From before the time of the patriarchs onward, the Bible presents a pluralistic picture, that is, different religions were part of its cultural context (Josh. 24:2). For centuries Christians in the eastern hemisphere have had to deal with adherents of other religions on a daily basis. Now globalization and increased immigration have brought widespread religious diversity to the West as well.

Peter's confrontational encounter with Simon Magus (or Simon the magician; see Acts 8:9-25) teaches that we must not surrender to the subtleties of religious relativism. Though relativistic pluralism is currently politically correct, it is also biblically inaccurate, spiritually bankrupt, theologically inept, and eternally inadequate. Contemporary Christians are called to bear clear and uncompromising witness to Jesus Christ as Lord and Savior, and to the truth of Holy Scripture as divinely inspired, authoritative revelation. The mandate and mission of the church is still to publish abroad the good news of the gospel of God's grace to all people everywhere (Matt. 28:19-20).

After acknowledging the *fact* of religious plurality, we must deal decisively with the fallacious *philosophy* of religious pluralism. Any idea that all religions are essentially equal or different yet valid paths to the same place is not only contrary to common sense but to the plain truth of the Bible (John 14:6; Acts 4:12). Without inconsiderate or intolerant pronouncements denigrating or damning others, evangelical believers should always testify to the centrality and necessity of Christ for knowing the true God and eternal life (John 17:3).

A pagan king of Babylon attempted unsuccessfully to undermine the religious faith and values of young Jews by blurring their identity through blending it with his own (Dan. 1:1-21). Evangelical Christians today need to guard against conceding too much to contemporary culture (whether religious or otherwise). "Religion that is pure and undefiled before God" is our constant goal (Jas. 1:27). That requires really knowing who we are, what we believe, and why. A Presbyterian-turned-Buddhist once told me he converted out of Christianity because his upbringing in the faith never became personally vital.

Being faithful Christians in a world of pluralistic faiths begins with being firmly rooted in our own rich religious heritage. A life of personal discipleship including prayer and Scripture reading in a context of active participation in a vibrant community of faith is absolutely essential for successfully navigating the multi-faith maze of modernity. Furthermore, an undiminished commitment to the lordship of Christ and an undiluted confidence in the anointing of the Holy Spirit equips us to overcome the almost daily assaults aimed at undermining our sense of Christian faith, life, strength, and truth. Our Pentecostal experience of the Holy Spirit is bold testimony to Jesus Christ beyond all boundaries into the entire earth (Acts 1:8; 2:4).

Evangelicals may well view the religious variety of our modern world as more of an opportunity than a problem. The apostle Paul used interreligious contact points to bridge barriers to introducing pagans to the Christian gospel (Acts 14:8-18; 17:22-23). We would do well to remember that many members of other religions are devout and pious people, at least according to their own spiritual standards. In my own interreligious encounters, I find it helpful to put into practice the following five important values: charity (love), hospitality, availability, certainty, and humility.

- *Charity* witnesses to religious others by letting the light of Christ's love shine through our words and deeds, not just generally but specifically toward those of other faiths (Luke 10:25-37).

- *Hospitality* in social interaction treats them as our neighbors-in-need rather than as religious rivals or eternal enemies, becoming a multifaceted means of God's grace (1 Pet. 4:9-10).

- *Availability* indicates that without pressuring or pushing we place ourselves at their disposal when they inevitably inquire about our belief (1 Pet. 3:15).

- *Certainty* stands strong for our deepest faith convictions, being upfront and unapologetic about what we believe (1 Cor. 14:8).

- *Humility* works hard at not coming across arrogantly as if we feel we have the final word on all divine truth; we can confess that we "know only in part" (1 Cor. 13:9).

Practicing these five values can bear witness to the truth and power of faith in Jesus Christ to those of other faiths.

At one interreligious dialogue event, a pleasant Jewish gentleman approached me for further discussion after my presentation. We talked repeatedly over the next few days. He admitted to having had a stereotypical picture of evangelicals as harsh, holier-than-thou people with narrow minds and hard hearts. He candidly confessed to being a bit confused by the "failure" of my wife and me to live down to his presumptions. He sincerely asked me to share my testimony. As I talked about how Jesus set me free from sin and the Holy Spirit filled me with joy, love, and power, I saw tears well up in his eyes. He was obviously and unashamedly moved deeply. He exclaimed that he had long desired and sought such an experience. Perhaps the best witness we offer the world and its many religions is just being faithful to the reality of our own holy heritage as Christians.

The incarnation of Christ is a unique, non-repeatable event. Theologian French Arrington writes that it is "a miracle of the most profound significance." C. S. Lewis said the incarnation is "the central event in the history of the Earth" and "the central point in Christianity." Religions such as Hinduism and Islam may make do without any miraculous elements. That is not the case with Christianity. Hinduism is mystical. Islam is natural. But Christianity is supernatural. It is "precisely the story of a great Miracle"! The incarnation is the Grand Miracle that sets the stage for everything else. Jesus did not inhabit a human body; he became a human being. God became flesh! Jesus is forever fully God and fully human. Through the incarnation, Christ revealed God (John 1:18), offered himself as a sacrifice for sin (Heb. 10:1-10), destroyed the works of the devil (1 John 3:8), became a merciful and faithful high priest (Heb. 2:17), and provided an example for holy living (1 Pet. 2:21). Hallelujah!

Often my personal interfaith encounters are genuinely enriching. I remember watching a young Hindu woman fuss like a mother hen over an elderly Jewish lady as we crammed into a crowded taxi rushing to the airport. Then there was the Pure Land Buddhist monk my wife describes as the gentlest and kindest soul she had ever met. We have never met more devout people nor been treated better than when we spent time in the home of a rabbi and her husband. I laughed a lot with a likable young Muslim clergyman, who said that he'd attended a Christian seminary just to get to know his new neighbors better. (Admittedly, a few times I have been upset or angered at interfaith events. I will not soon forget an elderly Sikh man who slyly suggested that identifying the "terrorists" depends largely on who ends up winning the war and writing its history. We were standing near Ground Zero on the third anniversary of 9/11.)

To tell the truth, I admire Moses' Holy Law and Mohammed's abhorrence of idolatry. I admire Confucius's relational wisdom, Buddha's compassion for sufferers, and Gandhi's sacrificial service for people. Of course, we Christians will disagree strongly with some of their beliefs. Yet we ought to esteem each of these individuals as outstanding human beings. However, Jesus Christ is more than an outstanding human being—much more (Matt. 12:41-42). He is our Savior and Lord. He is the Son of God and the Messiah.

Just what is so special about Jesus? What makes him so different from everyone else? Biblically, we may identify four activities underscoring the absolute and utter uniqueness of Jesus of Nazareth.

- *His revealing:* Jesus did not merely teach us about God but rather he unveiled for us in his own person the very character and nature of God (John 1:14, 18).
- *His reconciling:* In Jesus the enmity between God and humanity, and thus between humans beings, is removed and replaced with peace (2 Cor. 5:18).
- *His redeeming:* Jesus' atoning death on the cross liberates from sin and death, as well as delivers from all debilitating and dehumanizing forces, or demonic principalities and powers (Col. 2:13-15).
- *His reigning:* Jesus' resurrection from the dead and exaltation to the Father's right hand declares and demonstrates his divine authority and power (Acts 2:36).

These four features set Jesus apart from all ordinary religious founders, leaders, or teachers. Christians should appreciate and respect great men and women of other religions. Yet Jesus stands alone as supremely significant. Through the knowledge of him, we've been given "everything needed for life and godliness" (2 Pet. 1:3).

Many believe Christians are slowly but surely being backed into a corner. If we concede to religious pluralism, we surrender any semblance of biblical or historic Christian faith (which would be contrary to Jude 3). But if we contend for Christian uniqueness, we are portrayed as narrow and nasty, backward and bigoted fundamentalists. In many minds, we become comparable to the Taliban. What then are we to do? In my own interfaith experiences, I find employing the following core group of commitments surprisingly effective. These will serve well with family, friends, and fellow workers of different faiths also.

- Commitment to *the Word of God:* Our beliefs and practices must always align themselves with the teaching of Scripture rather than the pressure of culture. Proverbs 14:12 says, "There is a way that seems right to a person, but its end is the way to death." Accordingly, Christians cannot conscientiously affirm that all paths are equally right. We must always maintain the uniqueness of Christ and the necessity of faith in Christ.

- Commitment to *the witness of the Spirit:* The Spirit testifies within us regarding our right standing with God in Christ (Rom. 8:16-17). The Spirit also reaches out to all people everywhere (Num. 27:15). Accordingly, Christians can cautiously identify signs of God's gracious presence and influence beyond ecclesial or sectarian borders.

- Commitment to *the way of love:* Jonah knew the Lord is "a gracious and compassionate God, slow to anger and abounding in love" (4:2, NIV). Jonah balked at interacting with those he considered godless heathen and begrudged them God's love and mercy. However, God reproved the prophet's rashness (4:10-11). Accordingly, Christians can confidently bear witness of Christ in a religiously pluralistic world by treating religious others with Godlike love.

After Jesus' encounter with the Syrophoenician woman, he "left the vicinity of Tyre and went through Sidon, down to the Sea of Galilee and into the region of the Decapolis" (Mark 7:31, NIV). The Phoenician republic of Sidon was located on the coast, some twenty miles north of Tyre. Jesus apparently journeyed northward to Sidon and then turned southeastward along the eastern shore of the Sea of Galilee through a Hellenistic area known as the Decapolis. This means that Jesus remained for some time in territory with strong Gentile associations. Pagan country! Jesus' excursion beyond ancient Israelite borders was not a temporary jaunt. He was permanently committed to making contact with people outside traditional religious circles.

Will we join Jesus on an excursion beyond ancient borders? Will we commit to dialogue with and prayer for those of different cultures and faith backgrounds? Let Christians today search out seekers beyond the church. Like Jesus, may we recognize faith, wherever we find it, and respond to it with honest dialogue and powerful prayer for God's healing action. Amen.

Tony Richie is senior pastor at New Harvest Church in Knoxville, Tennessee, and a missionary teacher and adjunct professor. Additionally, he serves various ecumenical organizations, including with the Interfaith Relations Commission of the National Council of Churches USA, and on the advisory board of the World Council of Churches. Tony is author of *Speaking by the Spirit: A Pentecostal Model for Interreligious Dialogue.*

CONCLUSION

Let me close by repeating something I said at the beginning: This book is not a how-to manual for preaching, at least not primarily. If it were, it would have included a major section on how to craft a missional sermon. In lieu of that, I trust that the sermons following each chapter in Part 2 have given us an idea of what missional proclamation may sound like. I trust too that the summary principles with which each chapter concludes can serve as guidelines for those of us who by our preaching desire to mold our churches into the shape of God's mission. So although it is not a how-to manual, I hope this book serves the church in a practical way.

I do hope that, as preachers and teachers, we are always seeking to improve our craft. After all, which of us no longer needs to improve in our delivery, our clarity, our study habits, our time management, etc.? The appendix—a sermon evaluation form—is designed to help us assess our own sermons based on the missional standards set forth in these pages. But my larger hope is that God and God's mission will so flow through our bloodstream, and that we will fall so madly in love with the God who loved the world enough to send the only begotten Son, that our preaching cannot help but exude God's redeeming love for the world and everyone in it.

In truth, I set forth to write nothing less than a theology of mission, but one with preachers in mind. As a missiologist, I have shelves and shelves of books on God's mission, but strangely, not too many of them preach very well. And as a preacher, I also have shelves and shelves of commentaries and books on homiletics, but strangely, not too many of them are written as if the world matters. But the world *does* matter, so the study of mission must not be relegated to seminary halls and libraries alone. It must ultimately grab hold of pastors in the trenches, who in turn inspire the people of God under their care to engage the world in mission.

As we have seen, missional preaching requires us to embrace the powerful reality of the *missio Dei* wholeheartedly; it requires us to read the whole of the Bible from Genesis to Revelation with missional, kingdom eyes; and it requires us to incorporate mission in the regular worship experience of the church. Building on these three essentials, we looked closely at seven large goals that provide the contours of a missional church. Let me emphasize that these are large goals! Obviously, they cannot be accomplished in a week, a month, a year, ten years, or a hundred years. On the contrary, they represent a lifelong process and a lifetime of preaching.

Preaching is not everything, but it plays a central role in giving shape to the church in the world. In this book, I have diagnosed the American church today as essentially malnourished because it has not been fed with the thoroughly missional Word of God as it is encased in the pages of Scripture. I have argued that missional preaching can do its part to nourish the church back to health, as it causes the heart of God's people to beat in rhythm with God's heart for the lost and the poor, and as it cuts away excess fat and firms up the church's muscles for practical action. At the end of the day, that is the vision for which missional preaching strives: to see the people of God healthy, fit, and out of the pews, actively living out our faith in word and deed, with energy, confidence, and passion.

> *And now may the radical love and justice of God the Father, the liberating forgiveness of God the Son, and the transforming power of God the Holy Spirit so penetrate our lives that we go forth into this broken, unjust, unevangelized world and begin to change it; for the risen Jesus has already won the victory over sin, injustice, and even death itself. Hallelujah!*[1]

NOTE

1. I learned this inspiring holistic benediction from Ronald J. Sider, my colleague and mentor at Palmer Theological Seminary and Evangelicals for Social Action.

AFTERWORD

Much has been said and written about the missional church—and appropriately so, as it represents a refreshing direction for the faith at a time when many mainline denominations are becoming more and more inward- and self-focused. The adage is true that congregations are fond of calling themselves friendly, but visitors often experience them as friendly only with one another. Juxtaposed against the extended family concept of a particular church fortressed against the world comes the idea that the church's existence is to transform the world by bringing its resources to the task of eradicating economic, moral, and cultural injustice. In the missional church, ministry to the other becomes the primary objective of the church's witness and work.

Of course, if churches are to reach beyond their four walls and their comfort zones, they must have preachers and teachers who will promote that direction. Even the best theology of mission remains no more than an arrow in the quiver if it is never placed on the bow and directed toward a target. As Paul told the Corinthians, it is "through the foolishness of our proclamation" that God chose to save the world (1 Cor. 1:18-25).

Dr. Al Tizon has made a significant contribution to the church's understanding of its missional nature by setting down preaching as the primary vehicle through which this idea of church outreach is communicated. As Isaiah pronounced, "How beautiful upon the mountains are the feet of the messenger who announces peace, who brings good news, who announces salvation, who says to Zion, 'Your God reigns'" (Isa. 52:7). Paul built upon that and wrote, "How shall they hear without a preacher? And how shall they preach unless they are sent?" (Rom. 10:14-15, NKJV).

There are many books on the "how to" of preaching—how to outline, how to organize, how to illustrate, etc. Dr. Tizon sets down a very practical guide as to how to direct preaching toward the church's primary direction as set down in Matthew 28, "Go, therefore, into all the world. . . ." Dr. Tizon's voice is a clarion call to churches everywhere, and to preachers everywhere, that we must not keep the Good News as though it were a private club for key insiders. Instead, we must make the gospel available for all, as it was intended. It is only when this is done that the kingdoms of this world will become the kingdoms of our God and of his Christ.

Rev. Dr. Wallace Charles Smith
Senior Minister, Shiloh Baptist Church
Washington, DC
Dean, Smith School for Christian Ministry
Palmer Theological Seminary of Eastern University
Wynnewood, PA

Is It Missional?

A SERMON EVALUATION FORM

Scripture Text(s) _____

Sermon Title _____

1. In light of the assertion that the whole Bible is a missionary book, does the sermon adequately draw out the Scripture's missional dimension? Check the goals that apply:

___ *Inculturation:* Does it call the church to affirm and engage culture and/or cross cultures for the sake of the gospel?

___ *Alternative Community:* Does it call the church to be different from "the world"? Or more positively, how does it urge us to be loyal to the kingdom of God?

___ *Holistic Transformation:* Does it call people to personal growth or repentance? Does it challenge the church to works of evangelism, compassion, and justice?

___ *Justice and Reconciliation:* Does it challenge an injustice in the world, speak out for a marginalized group, or call for reconciliation across human divides?

___ *Whole-Life Stewardship:* Does it call the church to responsibility and generosity with regard to finances, material possessions, and/or the earth's resources?

___ *Life and Peace* (Shalom): Does it cry out against a destructive or violent practice or encourage life-affirming and peace-making ways?

___ *The Uniqueness of Christ* (Scandal of Jesus): Does it show respect to people of other faiths, while lifting up the name of Jesus Christ?

___ Other:

2. If the sermon does not draw out the missional dimensions of the text, how could it be revised to do so?

3. What, if any, specific course of action does the sermon lay out for the people of God?

4. Missional Effectiveness:

	Poor ... Excellent
The missional call came from the biblical text	1 2 3 4 5 6 7
It incorporated the good news of Jesus in a clear way	1 2 3 4 5 6 7
It was sensitive to gender and culture issues	1 2 3 4 5 6 7
Missional application was specific and doable	1 2 3 4 5 6 7
Overall rating of sermon from a missional perspective	1 2 3 4 5 6 7

Other comments:

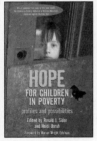

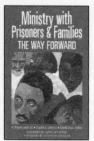

Ministry with Prisoners & Families: The Way Forward

Edited by W. Wilson Goode, Sr., Charles E. Lewis, Jr. and Harold Dean Trulear; Foreword by Addie Richburg.
Afterword by Dee Dee Coleman

"*Ministry with Prisoners and Families* will be important in helping to break the cycle of incarceration and recidivism, especially with its focus on the family as a critical element. This book provides a realistic, practical approach to addressing the problem of incarceration that will restore lives, reunite families, and rebuild communities. It is a must-read for churches, reentry programs, and the corrections community."

—Rev. Carmen Warner-Robbins, CEO and Founder, Welcome Home Ministries

"Its refreshing approach stands out in a sea of analysis that can often be enlightening but yet ineffectual. This is a highly recommended book for those who know the injustices at work in the prison system well enough to need no more convincing, and rather would seek to focus on what can be done now, a sense of urgency we could all use."

—Jason Wyman, *Fellowship* magazine

978-0-8170-1664-7 $17.99

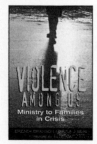

Violence among Us: Ministry to Families in Crisis

Brenda Branson and Paula J. Silva, Foreword by Tim Clinton

"Reading this book is like taking an intensive course on addressing domestic violence; a great deal of substance is compacted into a relatively small volume. The authors do an outstanding job of taking a reader without firsthand experience of abuse into the mind, body, and spirit of the abused, as well as that of the abuser. The feature that makes this book a stand-out is the comprehensive ready-to-use resource section. This book qualifies as a must-read for every pastoral, counseling, social work, or education student."

—*The Christian Librarian*

"...The best work to date available."

—Dr. Tim Clinton, President, American Association of Christian Counselors

978-0-8170-1515-2 $16.00

JUDSON PRESS | 800-458-3766 | www.judsonpress.com

Coming Together in the 21st Century:
The Bible's Message in an Age of Diversity
Curtiss Paul DeYoung; Foreword by Cain Hope Felder

"The change DeYoung has in mind is much more far-reaching, and much more powerful, than adding a praise song with a salsa beat or buying children's Bibles with multiracial pictures. DeYoung calls for Christians to preach a gospel fully freed from the colonial agenda of racism and privilege... *Coming Together in the 21st Century* is a prophetic book that rightly places the call to multiculturalism and liberation in the center of the gospel, and serves as a useful corrective to the myriad ways we still work and worship in a church warped by colonialism and its apologists."

—*Perspectives: A Journal of Reformed Thought*

978-0-8170-1564-0 $19.00

Reconciliation: Our Greatest Challenge – Our Only Hope
Curtiss Paul DeYoung

"A moral guide and practical road map through this difficult, painful, and ultimately liberating process called reconciliation."
—Jim Wallis, Editor-in-Chief, Sojourners

"Curtiss DeYoung deftly takes up the burning question of the church's potential leadership role in race relations and reminds us that meaningful change will cost something...A provocative but highly readable work about daring to make strangers and enemies begin to view one another as friends and equal members of the body of Christ."
—Cain Hope Felder, The Howard University School of Divinity

978-0-8170-1256-4 $15.00

JUDSON PRESS | 800-458-3766 | www.judsonpress.com